focus on florals

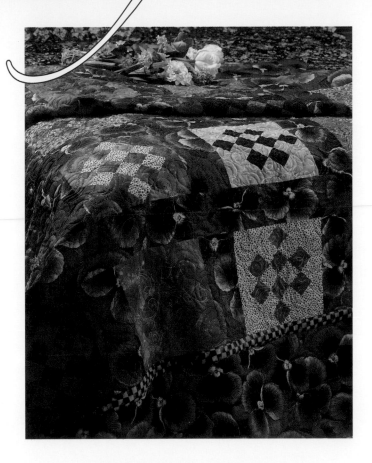

QUILTS FROM PRETTY PRINTS

TERRY MARTIN

Martingale® & COMPANY

Focus on Florals: Quilts from Pretty Prints
© 2005 by Terry Martin

That Patchwork Place® is an imprint
of Martingale & Company®.

Martingale & Company
20205 144th Avenue NE
Woodinville, WA 98072-8478 USA
www.martingale-pub.com

Printed in China
10 09 08 07 06 05   8 7 6 5 4 3 2 1

Library of Congress Cataloging-in-Publication Data
Martin, Terry.
　　Focus on florals / Terry Martin.
　　　　p. cm.
　　ISBN 1-56477-593-3
　1. Quilting—Patterns. 2. Patchwork—Patterns.
　3. Flowers in art. I. Title.
　　TT835.M273625 2005
　　746.46'041—dc22
　　　　　　　　　　　　　　　　　　　2004027883

Mission Statement
*Dedicated to providing
quality products
and service to
inspire creativity.*

Credits

President ❀ Nancy J. Martin

CEO ❀ Daniel J. Martin

VP and General Manager ❀ Tom Wierzbicki

Publisher ❀ Jane Hamada

Editorial Director ❀ Mary V. Green

Managing Editor ❀ Tina Cook

Technical Editor ❀ Dawn Anderson

Copy Editor ❀ Melissa Bryan

Design Director ❀ Stan Green

Illustrator ❀ Robin Strobel

Cover and Text Designer ❀ Regina Girard

Photographer ❀ Brent Kane

Dedication

I would like to dedicate this book to all the quilters who love this time-honored art form, to the fabric manufacturers that continue to make unbelievable prints, and to the quilt shops that support my habit (well, OK, shame on you!). Believe me, I could use some intervention on occasion.

I also dedicate this book to my younger brother, Stuart Cameron Maxwell, who died too young at the age of 40 from advanced multiple sclerosis. The quilt I made him will hang forever in my home.

Acknowledgments

Just like that old saying, "So much fabric, so little time," I have many people to offer my most sincere thanks to and probably not enough space to do it. But here goes. I am blessed with family, friends, and coworkers who are a constant source of inspiration, encouragement, support, and help, and who are always willing to share their opinions about my work. Cornelia, you are the "bestest" best friend that anyone could ask for, and I love you very much. Thanks for always being there. Regina, you are so sassy! Karen, you always have a solution to a problem. Robin, I love your ability to pick just the right fabrics. Tina, your unwavering support is so much appreciated. Thank you very much gals, you are the best!

I would like to especially recognize my machine quilters. They have taken my quilt tops and turned them into wonderful pieces of art, and they humble me with their artistic flair and talent. I love how they paint with thread. They are: my mentor and friend Barb Dau; "sure I can get that done for you in a week" Sue Lohse; "I can't wait to get my hands on that border!" Judy Irish; and "just let me show you what I can do with a huge floral print" Kathryn Milburn. (And she did.)

Many thanks also go to David Peha at Fabric Sales; The Erlanger Group; Woodrow Studio; and The Warm Company for their support in providing fabulous fabrics and products for this book.

Contents

Preface

This book is the result of a challenge I made to myself. I had just finished putting the final touches on my third book, *Snowflake Follies,* and although I loved working with all the wintry snowflake prints, I was looking for something new and "warm" to work on. I had inherited a bunch of floral fabrics in small pieces about 9" across, and of course I also had a number of florals in my stash. I went from winter snowflakes to summer florals in one day— I love quilting!

Now for the challenge: to design quilts that all focused on floral prints or used floral fabrics in the blocks or appliqué. It sounded simple enough, but I found myself really reaching and stretching my imagination to create fun quilts that were easy to make, stunning in appearance, and used lots and lots of small bits of floral fabrics.

This has been a very enjoyable, creative journey for me. I think these quilts represent some of my best work so far, and I hope you enjoy re-creating them. Here is my challenge to you: how about starting a small round-robin or block exchange among your quilting friends and work on quilts using only floral fabrics. Meet at your favorite quilt shop and pick up some lovely florals, selecting one for the feature fabric. Bring your floral stash, swap fabrics and ideas, pick a project from the book, and have fun!

Cheers! Terry

Introduction

The challenge I set for myself seemed simple: make all of the quilts from floral prints or floral blocks, or incorporate floral appliqué. I didn't realize how much I would need to know about fabric value and fabric scale. I confess that I am not artistically trained, and before writing this book, what I used to know about fabric value and scale could be summed up in a sentence or two. But, upon completion of this book and the projects within it, I can actually say that I have learned a lot.

In the first part of this book we will take a look at the importance of value and scale in choosing fabric for a project. My first rule of thumb is to audition, audition, audition. Trying out different fabrics has given me more success than anything else while designing quilts. The second rule is even simpler, and to quote my buddy Robin, it goes like this: "If it works for you, it works!"

The second part of this book is about the projects. I have created 11 projects for you to have fun with. I encourage you to use your own palette and make these quilts yours. I am surprised at the reaction I get when I lecture and tell my audience what I would change about a particular quilt if I were to do the project over again. It is hard for me to do the same thing twice, but that is the beauty of fabric—you can reuse the same quilt pattern but change the fabric's values, scale, and color, and you will have a quilt that is just as unique and individual as you are.

The third part of this book focuses on the nuts and bolts of quiltmaking, a general how-to reference on the mechanics of creating a quilt. Beginners can easily make most of these quilts, so this reference section is mostly for you. For the rest of you, refer to it for a quick refresher course as needed.

The Value of Value

The definition of value from a quilter's point of view is simple: value is the lightness or darkness of a color. It sounds simple enough, but it has a big impact on a quilter.

Value is the characteristic that creates depth in a quilt. As dark colors recede and light colors come forward, value can actually help you determine the design of a quilt block. The trickiest part of working with value in a quilt is that it is relative, shifting and changing as you add more fabrics. Just as there are lots of points on a compass between north, south, east, and west, so there are lots of points between the lightest white and the darkest black. To name just a few values, if you want to get very specific, there are light-light, light, medium-light, light-medium, medium-medium—you get the picture. Since values can vary so greatly, auditioning different fabrics side by side for color, scale, and print is important but not as crucial as evaluating them for a balance of value.

Notice how a fabric you label as a medium value can change when you compare it to other fabrics. Although a medium in one setting, it looks darker than a medium when you put it next to the lights, and the opposite is true when you look at it next to your dark fabrics.

The best method I know for determining the value of a fabric is to audition it with the other fabrics you are thinking of using. I lay out the fabrics in a fan formation from light to dark, or I might mix them up depending on which fabrics will be touching each other. I pull out and tuck in a number of fabrics until I am satisfied with the look, and then I walk away from it, coming back every so often to see if the array is still appealing. Looking at the collection of fabric from a distance will also help you find the balance of value you are looking for. If the fabric is too light it will glare out at you, while a fabric that is too dark may create a black hole that takes the life out of the quilt. By auditioning your fabrics you will be able to establish a balance of contrast that will give your quilt that extra punch.

Even with my audition process, I still occasionally tear out stitches and remove a fabric from a block and replace it with a different value. For example, the photo below shows an early version of "Autumn's Song" which appears on page 29. Notice how the green tone-on-tone fabric blends too much with the yellow print. It is a good color and works well with the rest of the fabrics, but the lack of contrasting value sent me back to my fabric stash to start over. The fabrics I decided to use instead include lots of warm colors and just enough contrast to be pleasing to the eye and give the quilt balance.

From light to medium to dark, the value of a fabric will change depending on the value of the fabric placed next to it.

The green and yellow prints lack contrast.

The best way for me to study and learn about the role of value in my quilt design work is, of course, by sight. Let's examine the simplest range of values: light, medium, and dark. Take a look at "Scrappy Lattice," below.

*This example shows distinct values:
light, medium, and dark.*

The cornerstones are the darks, the strippy 4" x 8" blocks are the mediums, and the large squares and four-patches are the lights. Notice how the pattern of the quilt is distinct because of these value changes. It reminds me of a garden lattice with the crisscross design and flowers peeking through to get to the sunshine. If you were to create this quilt using only one value, say medium, the result would look like a lot of pretty floral prints, but I can guess you would be hard-pressed to see the lattice pattern.

Now imagine switching the values in "Scrappy Lattice." Turn the lights into darks, the mediums into lights, and the cornerstones into mediums. Wow, what a difference! It is now midnight in the garden as the flowers are in shadow and the latticework bleaches against the moonlight.

*Changing value changes the
entire look of a quilt pattern.*

Another example of how value works in a quilt is seen in "Watercolor Irises," below. This quilt would be pretty using just the mediums and lights, but the addition of dark blue creates some visual punch.

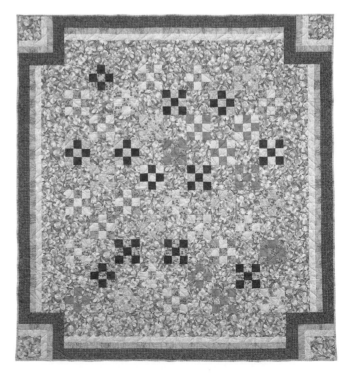

*Part of a fat-quarter pack, this dark blue has a
high-contrast value when used with lighter fabrics.*

When using spots of high-contrast fabric in a quilt, you can plan the placement carefully or arrange fabrics in a completely random fashion. When assembling "Watercolor Irises," I placed the Nine Patch blocks at random, so that the dark blue blocks are sprinkled here and there.

There are some tools that will help you assess value. The Ruby Beholder® is a dark red piece of plastic that can be used to view the relative values in fabric. When you look at your fabrics through the plastic, the colors disappear and you are left looking at shades of light to dark. It takes some practice, but using this tool can give you a real sense of the value of your fabrics. A reducing glass will also help. My friend Sondra went to the local home-improvement store and purchased a peephole like the one you would use on your front door. It reduces the detail of the fabrics so that you can concentrate on the value. I use the stand-away-from-the-fabric-and-squint method of testing for value. Looking through the "filter" of my eyelashes just seems to do the trick for me every time (well, almost every time).

Tools for determining value

Now, having examined the "value of value" and how it works in a quilt, you can throw everything I have said out the window and do what you want to do. I did! Check out "Black Beauty" on page 56. My challenge there was to make an entire quilt using only black-background floral prints. I did rely on the different values of the floral prints I used, and I am hoping you can see the overall design of this medallion quilt. One trend in quilting that is currently being explored is the blended quilt. Since the values are mostly the same, the quilt designer relies instead on the fabric print and color for subtle changes. So have fun playing and experimenting with value and do your own thing!

Take a moment to examine the quilt projects in this book for their use of value. With your discerning eye, you will be able to see what I was striving for in terms of value—and even, perhaps, what I could have done better!

Value plays an important part in this quilt where the dark baskets "pop" off the pastel backgrounds.

Fabric Scale

My first impulse is to say, "to learn about fabric scale, read about value," because evaluating scale is similar in many ways to evaluating value.

Let's back up a moment and define scale from a quilter's point of view. Scale is the size of the print on a piece of fabric. Scale can also include the size of a quilt block compared to the sizes of the other quilt blocks in a design.

I gladly blame the fabric manufacturers for expanding the scale of prints that are available to the quilter today. The range of scale in fabric prints goes far beyond the standard small, medium, and large. You can find everything from delicate miniprints (remember the pindot prints of the 1970s and '80s?) all the way through flower motifs the size of dinner plates.

These fabrics show a variety of scales, from miniprints to jumbo pansies.

Using a variety of scales in a quilt or quilt block creates movement. The eye can be wowed by the large, bold prints and then given a place to rest with smaller prints. Large-scale prints need more "breathing room" and are best suited for the larger pieces in a quilt block or for stand-alone borders. I think of large-scale prints the same way I view novelty prints: they need space to show off and coordinating fabrics to enhance their beauty. Take a look at "Passion Flower" on page 70. The pansy images can't get much bigger (they are the size of dinner plates!) and the colors of the print make a bold statement. When I was selecting the coordinating fabric, I had decided to include the pansy fabric for part of the quilt block. Wrong. The bold, large-scale print was so chopped up, it looked completely washed out next to the coordinating print. I did leave in one of the blocks using the pansy print, just to remind me that I learn something new every time I make a quilt.

The big, bold scale is lost in the small pieces of this quilt block.

I was pleased with the other fabrics I used, since the smaller scale of prints worked well with the "big boy" pansies.

Another balance of large and small scales is seen in "Autumn's Song" on page 27. As you know from the section on value, my first version of this quilt did not work, in more ways than one! Take a look at the scale of the fabrics in my first attempt, shown on page 8. The brown feature fabric has a medium- to large-scale print, but the print of the coordinating yellow fabric, although smaller, is too close in scale to the feature fabric. The results show a struggle for dominance between the two prints, and the last thing you want in a quilt is for the fabrics to struggle with each other! My final quilt has a much better balance; the feature fabric is larger in scale and the coordinating fabrics work well together. No struggles!

Have fun working with the wide range of print sizes available to choose from these days. Remember the pitfalls of using too large a print in a block that features lots of small pieces.

Tina's London

Finished quilt size: 25¼" x 25¼" ✿ **Finished block size:** 6¼"

*M*y coworker Tina traveled to London and brought me back a beautiful souvenir: a piece of Liberty of London fabric. It is so soft to the hand, with such rich color and design, I couldn't wait to use it in a quilt. The problem is I had only a 10½" width. Yikes! I generally make large quilts, so what was I going to do with it? After a bit of coaxing and hand-holding, I created a little cutie that is now one of my favorites, and I thank Tina for thinking of me while she was in London. But then again, if she had gone to London without bringing me back something, I'd have had a hard time speaking to her for a couple of weeks!

Tip The Liberty of London fabric is very lightweight, and I worried about how it would hold up while being paired with heavier, standard American cotton goods. My solution was to back the Liberty of London fabric with a lightweight fusible woven interfacing. It gave the fabric just enough "oomph" to piece with and stand up to the other cotton fabrics.

Materials

Yardage is based on 42"-wide fabric.

⅝ yard of floral print for alternate blocks and border

½ yard of blue print for blocks, border cornerstones, and binding

⅜ yard of cream print for blocks, inner border, and border cornerstones

30" x 30" piece of fabric for backing

30" x 30" piece of batting

Cutting

All measurements include ¼"-wide seam allowances.

From the cream print, cut:

❁ 1 strip, 3" x 42"; crosscut into 16 rectangles, 1¾" x 3"

❁ 20 squares, 2⅛" x 2⅛"; cut each square in half once diagonally to yield 40 half-square triangles

❁ 2 strips, 1½" x 18¼"

❁ 2 strips, 1½" x 20¼"

From the blue print, cut:

❁ 10 squares, 3⅜" x 3⅜"; cut each square in half once diagonally to yield 20 half-square triangles

❁ 24 squares, 1¾" x 1¾"

❁ 3 strips, 2½" x 42"

From the floral print, cut:

❁ 1 square, 6¾" x 6¾"

❁ 1 square, 10⅛" x 10⅛"; cut in half twice diagonally to yield 4 quarter-square triangles

❁ 2 squares, 5⅜" x 5⅜"; cut each square in half once diagonally to yield 4 half-square triangles

❁ 4 strips, 3" x 20¼"

Assembly

1. Sew cream print triangles to two adjacent sides of 20 blue print squares as shown.

Make 20.

2. Sew a blue print triangle to each unit from step 1 to make the corner units. Set aside four of the corner units for the cornerstones of the outer border.

Make 20.

***Tina's London** by Terry Martin. A special gift of fabric makes a lasting memory quilt.*

3. Sew corner units to opposite long edges of eight of the 1¾" x 3" cream print rectangles, orienting the corner units as shown.

 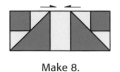

Make 8.

4. Sew the remaining 1¾" x 3" cream print rectangles to opposite sides of the remaining blue print squares to make the block center strips.

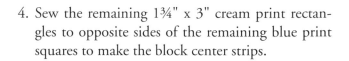  

Make 4.

5. Sew the units from step 3 to each side of the block center strips.

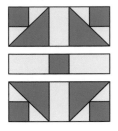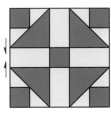

Make 4.

6. Sew the 10⅛" floral quarter-square triangles to opposite sides of two blocks.

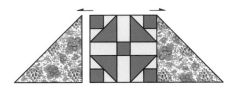

Make 2.

7. Sew a 5⅜" floral half-square triangle to the top of the units from step 6.

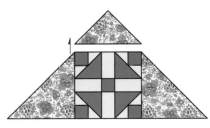

Make 2.

8. Sew the remaining two blocks to opposite sides of the floral square.

9. Sew the remaining 5⅜" floral half-square triangles to the ends of the unit from step 8.

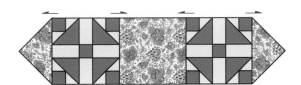

Make 1.

10. Sew the units from step 7 to opposite sides of the unit from step 9.

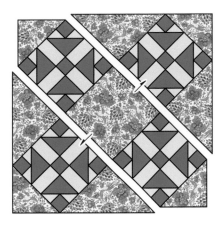

Borders

1. Sew the 1½" x 18¼" cream print inner-border strips to the sides of the quilt top. Press seam allowances toward the borders.

2. Sew the 1½" x 20¼" cream print inner-border strips to the top and bottom of the quilt top. Press seam allowances toward the borders.

3. Sew two of the 3" x 20¼" floral outer-border strips to the sides of the quilt top. Press seam allowances toward the floral borders.

4. Sew the four corner units that were set aside in step 2 of "Assembly" to the ends of the remaining floral outer-border strips, making sure to orient the cornerstones as shown.

Make 2.

5. Sew the pieced border strips to the top and bottom edges of the quilt top. Press seam allowances toward the inner border.

Quilt Assembly Diagram

Finishing

1. Make a quilt sandwich with the quilt top, batting, and backing; for more details on finishing techniques, refer to "Quiltmaking Basics" on page 72. Baste.

2. Quilt as desired. I machine quilted the design in the center of the quilt using a simple tulip motif from a purchased template. I stitched in the ditch around the block pieces, and the rest of the quilt has simple machine quilting inside the pieces. I used the edge of my walking foot as a guide and saved time by not having to mark the quilt!

3. Trim the batting and backing even with the edges of the quilt top. Add a hanging sleeve to your quilt if desired.

4. Sew the 2½" x 42" blue print strips together at right angles with a diagonal seam (see page 78) for the binding; sew the binding to the quilt and add a label.

Orange You Glad to See Me?

Finished quilt size: 74½" x 74½" ❀ **Finished block size:** 15"

I love rich fall colors, so the burnt orange floral fabric in this quilt is one of my favorites. I like this quilt block, as well, because it is like two blocks in one—the dark brown Shoo Fly, plus the pretty Flower block. This quilt design would look great in a number of different colorways, such as blue and yellow or burgundy and pink.

If you have the extra fabric, add a row of blocks on two adjacent sides; because the block is a hefty 15" square, you will have a queen-size quilt in no time.

Materials

Yardage is based on 42"-wide fabric.

2⅞ yards of orange floral print for blocks, outer border, and binding

2¾ yards of pale yellow print for blocks

1⅝ yards of green floral print for blocks and middle border

¾ yard of dark yellow print for blocks and inner border

¾ yard of brown print for blocks

5 yards of fabric for backing

79" x 79" piece of batting

Cutting

All measurements include ¼"-wide seam allowances.

From the pale yellow print, cut:

- ❀ 6 strips, 6½" x 42"; crosscut into 64 rectangles, 3½" x 6½"
- ❀ 4 strips, 3½" x 42"; crosscut into 64 rectangles, 2" x 3½"
- ❀ 17 strips, 2" x 42"; crosscut 13 of the strips into 256 squares, 2" x 2"

From the dark yellow print, cut:

- ❀ 4 strips, 2" x 42"
- ❀ 7 strips, 1½" x 42"

From the orange floral print, cut:

- ❀ 14 strips, 2" x 42"; crosscut into:
  64 rectangles, 2" x 3½"
  64 rectangles, 2" x 5"
- ❀ 8 strips, 5" x 42"
- ❀ 8 binding strips, 2½" x 42"

From the green floral print, cut:

- ❀ 7 strips, 5" x 42"; crosscut into 128 rectangles, 2" x 5"
- ❀ 7 strips, 2" x 42"

From the brown print, cut:

- ❀ 2 strips, 3½" x 42"; crosscut into 16 squares, 3½" x 3½"
- ❀ 4 strips, 3⅞" x 42"; crosscut into 32 squares, 3⅞" x 3⅞". Cut each square in half once diagonally to yield 64 half-square triangles.

Assembly

1. Sew the 2"-wide pale yellow print and dark yellow print strips together to make four strip sets. Cut 64 segments, 2" wide.

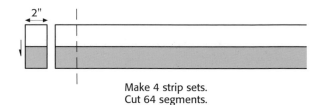

Make 4 strip sets.
Cut 64 segments.

2. Sew a 2" x 3½" pale yellow print rectangle to each segment from step 1.

Make 64.

Orange You Glad to See Me? *by Terry Martin. Quilted by Barbara Dau.*
A beautiful orange floral fabric called out to be used in this pretty quilt.

3. Draw a light pencil line diagonally from corner to corner on the wrong side of each 2" pale yellow print square.

Tip You may not need to mark the diagonal line on the squares since they are fairly small. In the next step, simply line up the diagonal corners on your sewing machine and sew a straight line.

4. Place a pale yellow print square right sides together on one end of each short and long orange floral rectangle. Sew from corner to corner as shown, paying attention to the correct angle of the stitching. Trim the seam to ¼" and press open.

Make 64.   Make 64.

5. Sew each short rectangle unit from step 4 to the side of a unit created in step 2.

Make 64.

6. Sew each long rectangle unit from step 4 to the bottom of a unit created in step 5.

Make 64.

7. Repeat step 4 with the green floral rectangles and the remaining pale yellow print squares, paying attention to the correct angle of the stitching.

Make 64.   Make 64.

8. Sew the units created in step 7 to adjacent sides of the block centers as shown.

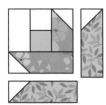 

Make 64.

9. Sew a brown print half-square triangle, right side down, across the remaining corner of each block, and trim ¼" from the stitching line as shown. Fold the triangles down and press to complete the flower units.

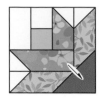 

Make 64.

10. Sew one 3½" x 6½" pale yellow print rectangle between two flower units as shown.

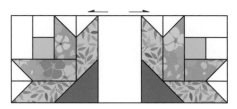

Make 32.

11. Sew the remaining 3½" x 6½" pale yellow print rectangles to opposite sides of the 3½" brown print squares.

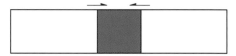

Make 16.

12. Sew the units created in step 10 to the top and bottom of the units created in step 11 to complete the blocks.

13. Sew the blocks into four rows of four blocks each. Sew the rows together.

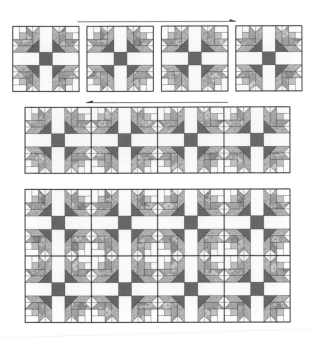

14. Sew the 1½" x 42" dark yellow print strips end to end. Following the instructions for "Straight-Cut Borders" on page 75, sew the yellow print inner border to the quilt top.

15. Repeat step 14 with the 2" x 42" green floral middle-border strips, and then with the 5" x 42" orange floral outer-border strips.

Finishing

1. Make a quilt sandwich with the quilt top, batting, and backing; for more details on finishing techniques, refer to "Quiltmaking Basics" on page 72. Baste.

2. Quilt as desired. My quilting friend Barb, who is also my quilt guild's president, did a fabulous job with the quilting. She used a variegated satin thread and really gave the flower petals lots of dimension. Her line quilting on other portions of the quilt made those areas recede to further the dimensional look. She's good!

3. Trim the batting and backing even with the edges of the quilt top. Add a hanging sleeve to your quilt if desired.

4. Sew the 2½" x 42" orange floral strips together at right angles with a diagonal seam (see page 78) for the binding. Sew the binding to the quilt and add a label.

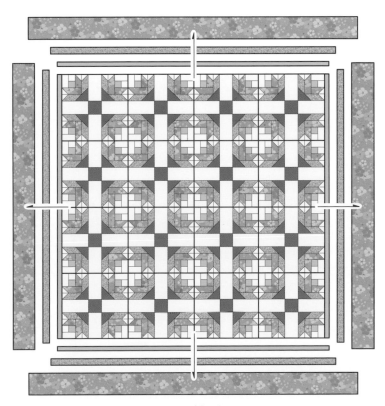

Quilt Assembly Diagram

Scrappy Lattice

Finished quilt size: 91¼" x 108¼" ✿ **Finished block sizes:** 4", 4" x 8", 8"

*T*his is one of the first quilts I made for Focus on Florals, *and in many ways it triggered me to write this book in the first place. My challenge was this: I had acquired a large amount of floral prints ranging from ⅛-yard cuts up to about ½-yard cuts, and these fabrics included a wide range of colors, designs, and prints. Some fabrics were several years old while others were more recently purchased; they were all very pretty. I wanted to work all of them into a quilt.*

The solution: a scrappy quilt. One nice feature of a scrappy quilt is not having to worry so much about color and scale. I just needed to concentrate on value with this quilt. I separated the fabrics into several piles: dark, a range of mediums and lights, and very light. The vast quantities of fabric worked perfectly for a scrappy quilt—when I ran out of one fabric, I simply grabbed another one and went back to work.

Materials

Yardage is based on 42"-wide fabric.

5¾ yards total of assorted medium floral prints for strip blocks

5 yards total of assorted light floral prints for center blocks and setting triangles

1⅜ yards total of assorted dark floral prints for cornerstones

8½ yards of fabric for backing

1 yard of blue print for binding

96" x 113" piece of batting

Cutting

All measurements include ¼"-wide seam allowances.

From the light floral prints, cut:

- ❀ 50 squares, 8½" x 8½"*

- ❀ 5 squares, 18¼" x 18¼"; cut each square in half twice diagonally to yield 20 quarter-square triangles (You will use 18 and have 2 left over.)

- ❀ 2 squares, 12¼" x 12¼"; cut each square in half once diagonally to yield 4 half-square triangles

From the medium floral prints, cut:

- ❀ Strips ranging from 1" to 2½" wide x the length of the fabric. Sort the strips into groups of approximately the same length. The length needs to be a minimum of 5", because you will be cutting 4½" x 8½" rectangles from the strips once they are sewn together.

From the dark floral prints, cut:

- ❀ 71 squares, 4½" x 4½"

From the blue print, cut:

- ❀ 11 strips, 2½" x 42"

*These squares can be a combination of 8½" squares cut from a single fabric and 8½" blocks pieced from four different fabric squares. If you have only small scraps of fabric, a pieced Four Patch block makes good use of your scraps. Determine how many of your squares will be made from Four Patch blocks, and then cut four 4½" squares for each block. Cut 8½" squares for the remaining blocks.

Assembly

1. If you planned to use Four Patch blocks for some of your 8½" squares, randomly select four 4½" squares of light floral and sew them together. You will need a total of fifty 8½" squares.

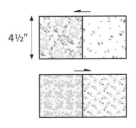

Scrappy Lattice *by Terry Martin. Quilted by Sue Lohse. A trellis garden of floral fabrics*
set on point is a romantic quilt for the master bedroom or guest room.

2. Randomly select from the medium floral strips of similar lengths and sew them together to make strip sets. Make sure that each set measures at least 5½" x 9½" (you'll be cutting 4½" x 8½" units from the sets). Press the seam allowances in one direction.

Making the strip sets wider than necessary gives you the opportunity to make adjustments when cutting out the sashing units. You can position your ruler along the strip to avoid a very skinny piece of fabric at either end of the unit.

3. From the strip sets, cut as many 4½" x 8½" sashing units as will fit across the strips. You will need a total of 120 units.

8½"

4½"

Make 120.

4. Sew the 4½" dark floral squares to the strip-pieced sashing units, alternating the squares and sashing units to make sashing rows as shown in the quilt assembly diagram on page 26. Make two rows that have a total of two dark squares, two rows that have four dark squares, two rows that have six dark squares, two rows that have eight dark squares, two

rows that have ten dark squares, and one row that has eleven dark squares.

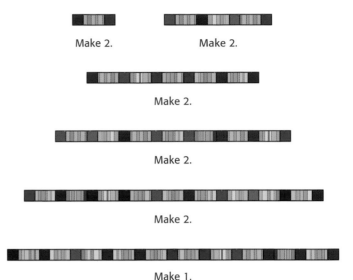

Make 2.   Make 2.

Make 2.

Make 2.

Make 2.

Make 1.

5. Sew the remaining strip-pieced sashing units to the sides of the 8½" squares and Four Patch blocks as shown.

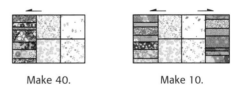

Make 40.   Make 10.

6. Sew the units from step 5 together to create the rows as shown.

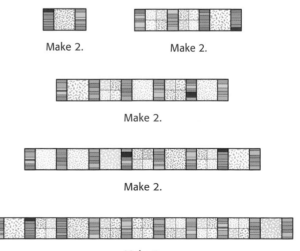

Make 2.   Make 2.

Make 2.

Make 2.

Make 2.

7. On the top of each row created in step 6, sew the corresponding sashing strip created in step 4. Press the seam allowances toward the sashing strips.

8. Sew the light floral quarter-square triangles to each end of the rows created in step 7, referring to the quilt assembly diagram as a guide for proper placement. Press the seam allowances toward the triangles.

9. Sew the rows together as shown in the quilt diagram.

10. Sew the light floral half-square triangles to each corner of the quilt. Press the seam allowances toward the triangles.

Finishing

1. Make a quilt sandwich with the quilt top, batting, and backing; for more details on finishing techniques, refer to "Quiltmaking Basics" on page 72. Baste.

2. Quilt as desired. Sue Lohse created a meandering pattern of simple floral motifs.

3. Trim the batting and backing even with the edges of the quilt top. Add a hanging sleeve to your quilt if desired.

4. Sew the 2½" x 42" blue print strips together at right angles with a diagonal seam (see page 78) for the binding. Sew the binding to the quilt and add a label.

Quilt Assembly Diagram

Autumn's Song

Finished quilt size: 30¼" x 30¼" ✿ **Finished block size:** 21"

*M*any of my coworkers share a great passion for quilting—we talk about quilts, share ideas, problem-solve, and have a wonderful working relationship. Some of my favorite quilt retreats are with these very talented women.

This quilt is a great example of sharing ideas. Karen Costello Soltys came up with this quilt design and I just loved it. She enlarged the traditional Christmas Star block, set it on point, and surrounded it with a fabulous floral print. Her quilt appears in the gallery of quilts in Triangle Tricks (Martingale & Company, 2003), but no pattern was given. So I'm happy to show my version here, complete with instructions for making your own.

The quilt top can be completed in an afternoon and is a great way to show off a beautiful medium- or large-scale floral print.

Materials

Yardage is based on 42"-wide fabric.

1⅛ yards of medium- to large-scale floral print for block, border, and binding

⅜ yard of pink floral print for block background

¼ yard or scraps of green print for block

¼ yard or scraps of yellow floral print for block

¼ yard or scraps of dark rust print for block

35" x 35" piece of fabric for backing

35" x 35" piece of batting

Cutting

All measurements include ¼"-wide seam allowances.

From the yellow floral print, cut:

❀ 2 squares, 4¾" x 4¾"; cut each square in half twice diagonally to yield 8 quarter-square triangles

From the medium- to large-scale floral print, cut:

❀ 1 square, 7½" x 7½"

❀ 2 squares, 5⅞" x 5⅞"; cut each square in half once diagonally to yield 4 half-square triangles

❀ 4 squares, 3" x 3"

❀ 2 squares, 15¾" x 15¾"; cut each square in half once diagonally to yield 4 half-square triangles

❀ 4 strips, 2½" x 42"

From the pink floral print, cut:

❀ 8 squares, 4⅜" x 4⅜"; cut each square in half once diagonally to yield 16 half-square triangles

❀ 8 squares, 4" x 4"

From *each* of the green print and dark rust print fabrics, cut:

❀ 4 squares, 4⅜" x 4⅜"; cut each square in half once diagonally to yield 8 half-square triangles (16 total)

Assembly

1. Sew yellow floral triangles to two adjacent sides of each 3" floral print square as shown.

Make 4.

2. Sew a 5⅞" floral half-square triangle to each unit from step 1.

Make 4.

Autumn's Song *by Terry Martin. The rich colors and different*
values of this little one-block quilt make it really stand out.

3. Sew two pink floral half-square triangles and two dark rust print half-square triangles to adjacent sides of each unit created in step 2. Press seam allowances toward the triangles.

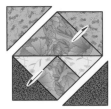 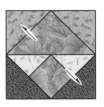

Make 4.

4. Sew two of the units from step 3 to opposite sides of the 7½" floral square as shown.

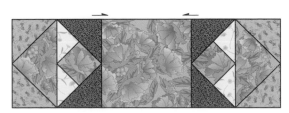

Make 1.

5. Sew the green print triangles to the remaining pink floral triangles to make eight half-square-triangle units.

Make 8.

6. Sew each half-square-triangle unit to a 4" pink floral square, and sew the resulting units together in pairs as shown.

Make 8.   Make 4.

7. Sew the units from step 6 to opposite sides of the remaining units created in step 3 as shown.

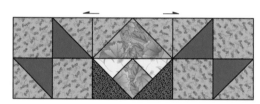

Make 2.

8. Sew the units from step 7 and the unit created in step 4 together as shown.

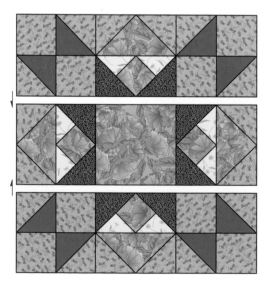

Make 1.

9. Sew the remaining floral half-square triangles to each side of the block created in step 8. Press seam allowances toward the triangles.

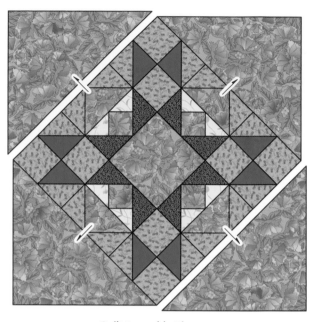

Quilt Assembly Diagram

Finishing

1. Make a quilt sandwich with the quilt top, batting, and backing; for more details on finishing techniques, refer to "Quiltmaking Basics" on page 72. Baste.

2. Quilt as desired. I added some curved machine quilting to this piece to take some of the edge off of all the squares and triangles. The radiating quilting lines in the large outside triangles were easy and fun to do.

3. Trim the batting and backing even with the edges of the quilt top. Add a hanging sleeve to your quilt if desired.

4. Sew the 2½" x 42" floral strips together at right angles with a diagonal seam (see page 78) for the binding. Sew the binding to the quilt and add a label.

Antique Cutie

Finished quilt size: 52½" x 68½" ❀ **Finished block sizes:** 4" and 12"

*M*y coworker Robin brought in an old quilt catalog from the 1920s, a treasure that her sister sent to Robin after finding it in their mother's attic. (Don't you just love those kinds of discoveries?) We marveled at how inexpensive the items were back then, but I wasn't looking at the prices—a little antique cutie of a block was staring back at me from the brittle, aged page. It quietly said, "Make me." And I said, "I will." But wait a minute, I do NOT appliqué! Double-backed fusible web to the rescue! This is when I created my own new word for the quilting industry: applifuse. I love the look of appliqué, and someday when I slow down a bit, I will take needle in hand and appliqué; but until then, fusible web and my sewing machine's decorative stitches are all I need.

This quilt is a great way to put your fabric scraps to work. I used a lot of floral fabrics that were getting a little tired-looking sitting in my stash. These are fabrics I bought several years ago that just weren't right for the projects I had been working on. But when I put them together with other fabrics, all of a sudden they gained a new life. Although it looks it, this project doesn't rely on any of the reproduction prints that are available now, but it would look great if you used them.

Materials

Yardage is based on 42"-wide fabric.

2½ yards of printed muslin for block backgrounds, sashing strips, and corner blocks

2⅜ yards total of scraps or small yardages of assorted floral prints for block designs, sashing strips, and corner blocks

3½ yards of fabric for backing

⅝ yard of floral print for binding

57" x 73" piece of batting

Steam-A-Seam 2 fusible web (three packages, each 12" x 1 yard)

Cutting

All measurements include ¼"-wide seam allowances.

From the printed muslin, cut:

❋ 6 strips, 12½" x 42"; crosscut into:
  12 squares, 12½" x 12½"
  31 rectangles, 2½" x 12½"

❋ 4 strips, 1½" x 42"; crosscut into 80 squares, 1½" x 1½"

From the assorted floral prints, cut:

❋ 62 rectangles, 1½" x 12½"

❋ 20 squares, 2½" x 2½"

❋ 80 rectangles, 1½" x 2½"

❋ Trace 144 of the bay leaf template (page 36) onto the Steam-A-Seam 2. Remove the paper liner without the markings. Adhere the templates to the backs of as many fabrics as you like. Cut the bay leaves from the fabrics on the marked lines.

From the floral print for binding, cut:

❋ 7 strips, 2½" x 42"

Assembly

1. On the front of each 12½" printed muslin square, use a pencil to lightly draw a grid of lines as shown.

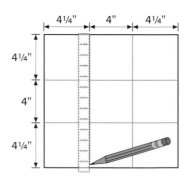

Antique Cutie by *Terry Martin. The antique block gives today's fabrics a vintage look. It's a pretty quilt to snuggle under for a summer nap.*

2. Remove the remaining paper liner of the Steam-A-Seam 2 from the bay leaf cutouts and center the bay leaves over the penciled lines as shown.

Make 12.

3. When all of the bay leaves are in place, follow the manufacturer's directions to fuse them to the printed muslin. Outline the leaves with a decorative machine buttonhole stitch.

 To prevent pillowing in the center of the block, I stitched the center curves first, then moved to the outside of the block.

4. Randomly select the 1½" x 12½" floral rectangles and sew them to each long side of the 2½" x 12½" printed muslin rectangles to make sashing units.

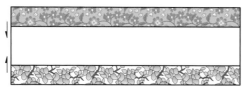

Make 31.

5. Randomly select the 1½" x 2½" floral rectangles and sew them to opposite sides of each 2½" floral square.

Make 20.

6. Sew a 1½" printed muslin square to opposite ends of each of the remaining 1½" x 2½" floral rectangles.

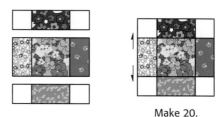

Make 40.

7. Sew a unit from step 6 to opposite sides of each unit created in step 5.

Make 20.

8. Sew each 4½" square block created in step 7 to one end of 15 sashing units created in step 4. On five of these units, sew a remaining 4½" square block to the opposite end.

Make 15.

Make 5 from the 15.

9. To make the sashing rows, sew two sashing units, each with one 4½" end block, and one sashing unit with two 4½" end blocks together end to end.

Make 5.

10. Sew a sashing unit made in step 4 to one side of each quilt block. On four of these units, sew another sashing unit to the opposite side.

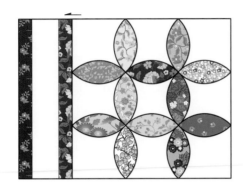

Make 12.

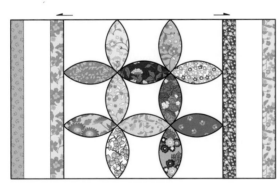

Make 4.

11. Sew two blocks, each with one sashing unit, and one block with two sashing units together to make a row. Make four.

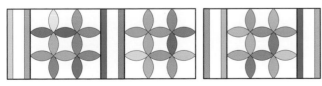

Make 4.

12. Sew a sashing row from step 9 to the top of each row of blocks created in step 11.

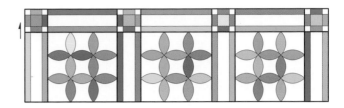

13. Referring to the quilt assembly diagram, sew the block and sashing rows together, adding the last row of sashing to the bottom.

Quilt Assembly Diagram

Finishing

1. Make a quilt sandwich with the quilt top, batting, and backing; for more details on finishing techniques, refer to "Quiltmaking Basics" on page 72. Baste.

2. Quilt as desired. I quilted in the ditch all along the straight edges and then stitched closely around the block motif. I traced the bay leaf shape in the blocks using a hera marker in the open space of the muslin rectangle and machine stitched on top of the hera markings. A hera marker is a plastic tool that leaves an indentation in the fabric rather than a mark as a pencil does. You need to quilt over the indentation fairly quickly before the fabric relaxes.

3. Trim the batting and backing even with the edges of the quilt top. Add a hanging sleeve to your quilt if desired.

4. Sew the 2½" x 42" floral strips together at right angles with a diagonal seam (see page 78) for the binding. Sew the binding to the quilt and add a label.

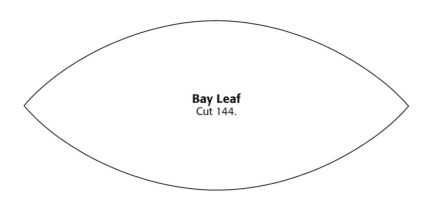

Bay Leaf
Cut 144.

Watercolor Irises

Finished quilt size: 78½" x 84½" ✿ **Finished block size:** 6"

*T*he feature fabric in this quilt reminds me of my grandmother's garden. She grew prize-winning bearded irises among a number of flowers she grew for pleasure and competition. She was a distinguished member of the Rose Society, in which she "rose" through the ranks and became a judge.

I love fat quarter packs, especially when the quilt shops put them together. The shops take away the guessing game of picking fabrics that complement each other. I belong to a fat quarter club, and each month I receive fat quarters of eight coordinating fabrics in the mail from Pincushion Boutique in California. The owner calls them Sweet Treats, and I couldn't agree more. They are my treat to myself.

This quilt contains one of those Sweet Treat fat quarter packs with additional yardage of the feature fabric. This fat quarter pack contained a nice range of light, medium, and dark fabrics. The dark fabric adds some kick to the simple design. I chose completely different fabrics for the borders, just to add a little extra sparkle. This is a fun, fast, and very easy quilt to make. I like how the Nine Patch blocks seem to float among the irises.

Materials

Yardage is based on 42"-wide fabric.

3⅜ yards of iris print for blocks and border

8 coordinating fat quarters for blocks

1¼ yards of green tone-on-tone fabric for border and binding

⅝ yard of purple tone-on-tone fabric for border

⅝ yard of yellow tone-on-tone fabric for border

⅝ yard of blue tone-on-tone fabric for border

8 yards of fabric for backing

83" x 89" piece of batting

Cutting

All measurements include ¼"-wide seam allowances.

From *each* of the fat quarters, cut:

❖ 7 strips, 2½" x 18"; crosscut into 45 squares, 2½" x 2½" (360 total; you will use 355 and have 5 left over)

From the iris print, cut:

❖ 4 strips, 2½" x 42"; crosscut into 50 squares, 2½" x 2½"

❖ 15 strips, 6½" x 42"; crosscut 9 of the strips into 49 squares, 6½" x 6½"

From *each* of the yellow, green, blue, and purple tone-on-tone fabrics, cut:

❖ 8 strips, 2" x 42" (32 total)

❖ 1 extra strip, 2" x 42", from the purple tone-on-tone fabric

From the remaining green tone-on-tone fabric, cut:

❖ 9 strips, 2½" x 42"

Assembly

1. For the Nine Patch blocks, randomly pair four squares of one fat quarter fabric with five squares from another and sew them together. Make 34. Also make five blocks by pairing four iris print squares with five fat quarter squares, and six more blocks by pairing five iris print squares with four fat quarter squares as shown.

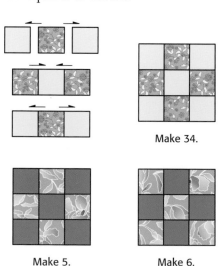

Make 34.

Make 5.   Make 6.

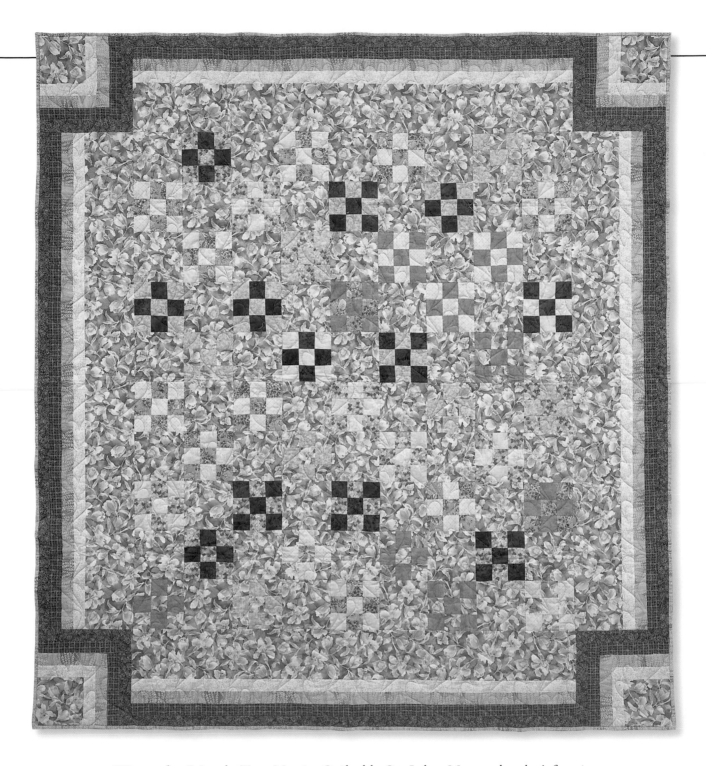

Watercolor Irises *by Terry Martin. Quilted by Sue Lohse. My grandmother's favorite flower was the bearded iris, and her garden was full of every color imaginable. As a child I thought the bearded petal was a tongue sticking out at me!*

2. Sew five each of the Nine Patch blocks and the iris fabric squares together to make vertical columns.

Make 9.

3. Arrange the vertical columns so that alternating columns begin with an iris square. Sew the columns together.

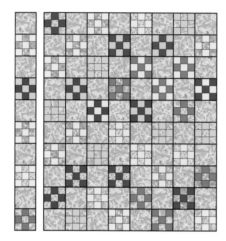

4. Sew a yellow tone-on-tone strip to one side of a remaining 6½" iris square, trimming the strip even with the edges of the iris square. Repeat to add yellow to an adjacent side of the square. Repeat this step with the green, blue, and purple tone-on-tone strips to complete the modified Log Cabin block for the quilt corners.

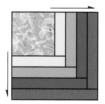

Make 4.

5. Sew the remaining yellow tone-on-tone strips together end to end. Repeat with the green, blue, and purple tone-on-tone strips and the iris strips.

6. Sew the iris strip and the yellow, green, blue, and purple strips together in that order to make a long strip set.

7. Crosscut the strip sets into two 60½" segments and two 54½" segments to make border strips.

8. Sew the 60½" border strips to the side edges of the quilt. Press seam allowances toward the borders.

9. Sew the corner blocks created in step 4 to each end of the remaining border strips, being careful to position the corner blocks as shown.

10. Sew these border strips to the top and bottom edges of the quilt top.

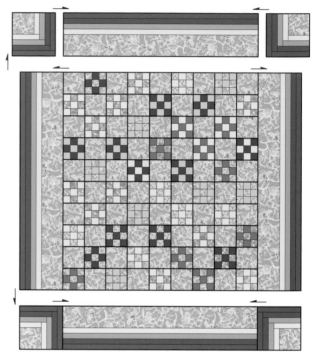

Quilt Assembly Diagram

Finishing

1. Make a quilt sandwich with the quilt top, batting, and backing; for more details on finishing techniques, refer to "Quiltmaking Basics" on page 72. Baste.

2. Quilt as desired. I had this project quilted with a lazy allover design. I wanted the quilting to allow the fluidity of the watercolor iris fabric to show through while adding extra dimension to the quilt as well.

3. Trim the batting and backing even with the edges of the quilt top. Add a hanging sleeve to the quilt if desired.

4. Sew the 2½" x 42" green tone-on-tone print strips together at right angles with a diagonal seam (see page 78) for the binding. Sew the binding to the quilt and add a label.

Still Life

Finished quilt size: 20½" x 27¼"

I love the look of the still life paintings by the old masters. They are graceful, beautiful, and rich with color and composition. I took a little more modern approach to a still life, and I hope I haven't offended the masters too much!

This little quilt was a lot of fun to design and make. My inspiration for the background came from a piece of fabric I had picked up along the way, in which blocks of prints were put together like a straight-lined puzzle. I worked my background pieces so there are no inset seams, and even though it looks complicated, it's not! And of course I took all the sophistication right out of the quilt by using eye-popping brights for the still life vase of flowers, turning it into a whimsical look that's just right for adding a little pizzazz to a room.

I also enhanced the resemblance to a still life image by quilting straight vertical lines in the background to look like wallpaper and a crisscross pattern below the vase to suggest a quilted tabletop.

The background pieces for this quilt are scraps in varying sizes, with the smallest measuring 3½" x 4½" and the largest 8½" x 10½". This gives you lots of freedom, so have fun picking through the scrap bin in your favorite fabric store or digging into your stash. I hope you enjoy creating your still life as much as I did.

Materials

Yardage is based on 42"-wide fabric.

¾ yard *total* of scraps of 10 or more white or light-background floral prints for quilt background. The prints should represent a variety of scales, and the colors should blend well, with no one fabric standing out much more than the others.

Scraps or fat eighths of the following tone-on-tone brights for vase, flowers, and greenery: blue, red, dark red, yellow, dark yellow, purple and green

25" x 32" piece of fabric for backing

⅜ yard of fabric for binding*

25" x 32" piece of batting

Steam-A-Seam 2 fusible web (1 package, 12" x 1 yard)

*I used a full fat quarter of the blue tone-on-tone fabric, cutting multiple 2½"-wide strips for the binding.

Cutting and Assembly

Starting with the background fabrics, make the following cuts and arrange the pieces in the positions shown on the diagram on page 44. Having a design area will help you greatly when auditioning the scraps for the different pieces of the background.

❀ 2 rectangles, 3½" x 5½"

❀ 2 rectangles, 6½" x 8½"

❀ 2 squares, 4½" x 4½"

❀ 3 rectangles, 3½" x 4½"

❀ 2 rectangles, 3½" x 6½"

❀ 2 rectangles, 5½" x 9½"

❀ 1 rectangle, 4½" x 10½"

❀ 1 rectangle, 8½" x 10½"

❀ 1 rectangle, 4½" x 7½"

❀ 1 rectangle, 4½" x 6½"

❀ 1 rectangle, 4½" x 12½"

Still Life *by Terry Martin. This wildly colored vase of flowers on a more subtle pieced background is a perfect wall hanging to really jazz things up.*

To assemble the background, follow these instructions.

1. Sew pieces 1–4 together as shown in the diagram.

2. Sew pieces 5–11 together as shown in the diagram.

3. Sew the unit from step 1 to the unit from step 2 as shown in the diagram.

4. Sew pieces 12 and 13 together, and then add this unit to the bottom of the unit created in step 3.

5. Sew pieces 14–18 together as shown in the diagram, and then add this unit to the right side of the unit created in step 4 to complete the background of the quilt top.

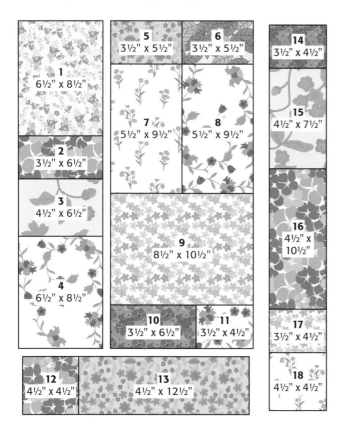

Adding the Appliqués

1. Using the vase, flower, and leaf patterns on pages 46–47, trace the number of motifs indicated onto the Steam-A-Seam 2. To save fabric and Steam-A-Seam 2, trace motifs meant for the same fabric in groups, leaving ¼" between each shape. Then cut out each group.

2. Remove the liner paper without the markings from each group. Following the manufacturer's directions, adhere the traced motifs to the back of the appropriate fabrics, and then cut them out on the marked lines.

3. Remove the remaining liner paper from the appliqué pieces. Starting with the vase, arrange the appliqué pieces on the quilt top as indicated in the diagram. Feel free to rearrange the flowers to your liking! The beauty of Steam-A-Seam 2 is that you can reposition the pieces as much as necessary without them flying off the design area. Once everything is placed to your satisfaction, fuse the motifs to the background, following the manufacturer's directions.

Tip Since this quilt is intended as a wall hanging, the permanent bond that Steam-A-Seam 2 provides will be adequate; stitching down the appliqué motifs is not necessary. This allows the flowers and vase to blend a little more with the background, enhancing the watercolor look. However, I chose to make the designs "pop out" of the background by using my sewing machine's buttonhole stitch and black thread. This way the piece is also washable if need be. Please feel free to experiment with decorative threads and machine or hand stitches to enhance the edges of the flower and vase appliqués.

Finishing

1. Make a quilt sandwich with the quilt top, batting, and backing; for more details on finishing techniques, refer to "Quiltmaking Basics" on page 72. Baste.

2. Quilt as desired. As mentioned before, I wanted to create the feel of a still life in this quilt. Using blue painter's tape, I created a vertical grid with two stitching lines close together, then a gap the width of the painter's tape, then two stitching lines close together to achieve the look of wallpaper in the background—you get the picture (ooh, sorry for the pun). For the look of a tabletop, I used the same blue painter's tape and created a slanted grid.

3. Trim the batting and backing even with the edges of the quilt top. Add a hanging sleeve to your quilt if desired.

4. Cut your binding fabric into 3 strips, 2½" x 42", or, if using a fat quarter for your binding, cut it into multiple strips, 2½" wide. Sew the strips together at right angles with a diagonal seam (see page 78). Sew the binding to the quilt and add a label.

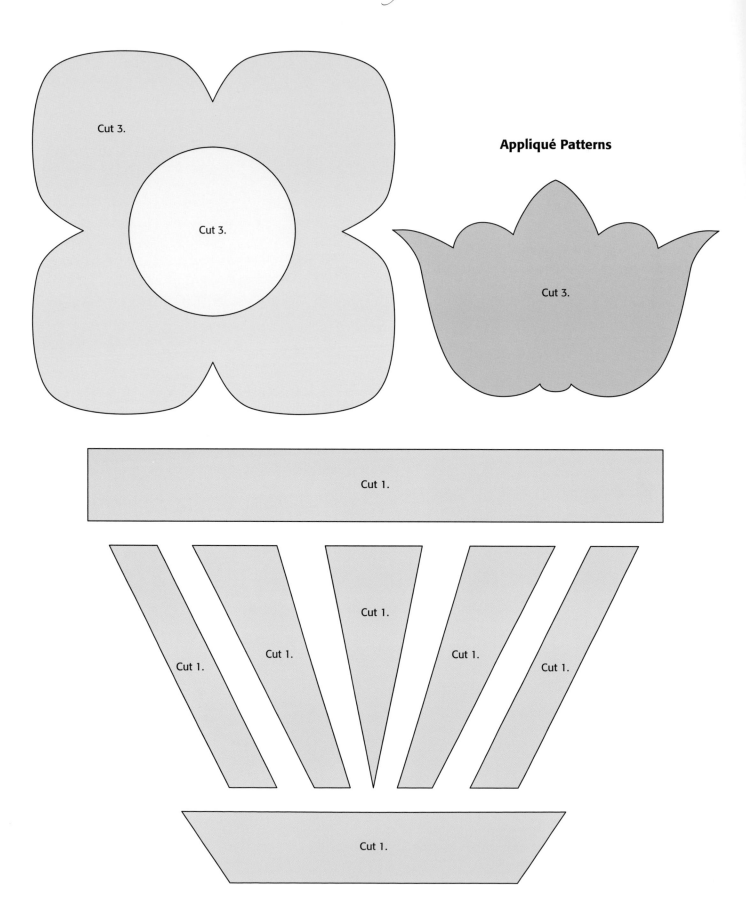

Appliqué Patterns

Cut 3.

Cut 3.

Cut 3.

Cut 1.

Cut 1.

Cut 1.

Cut 1.

Cut 1.

Cut 1.

Cut 1.

Appliqué Patterns

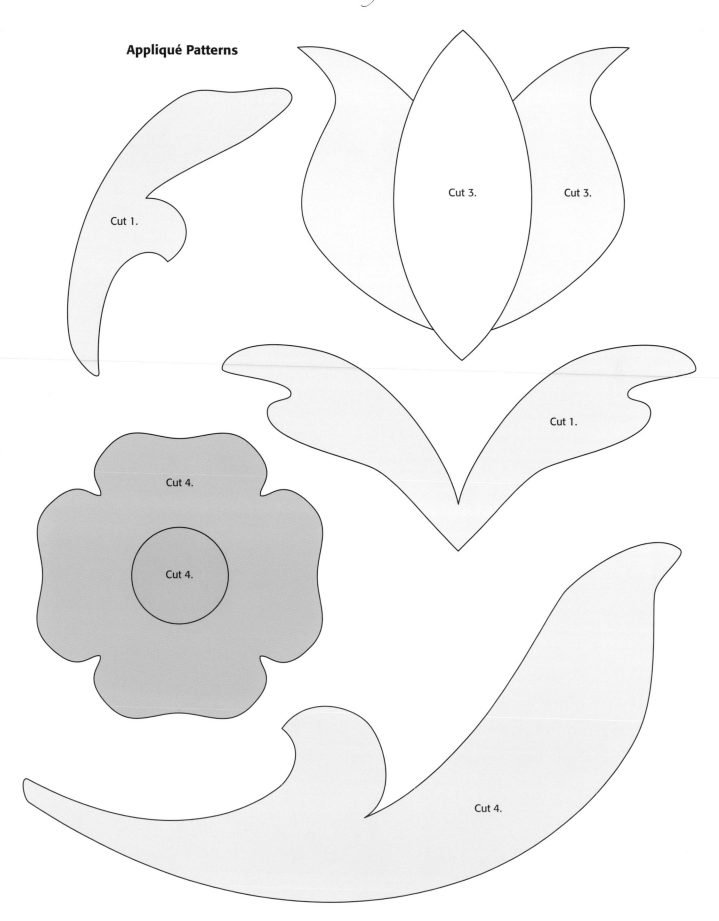

Cut 1.

Cut 3.

Cut 3.

Cut 1.

Cut 4.

Cut 4.

Cut 4.

Baskets of Flowers

Finished quilt size: 66¾" x 84½" ✿ **Finished block size:** 12½"

I feel especially touched when a quilt comes from a community effort. It demonstrates the strength and creativity of women and men when they share their talents. This is one of those quilts, and one of my favorites because of the community effort behind it. I work with a great bunch of people and most of us quilt. We have block exchanges on a pretty regular basis, and this quilt was created from one of those exchanges. My request was that each block use a floral in the center, a coordinating color for the basket, and a pastel for the background. From 14 women and one man I received these beautiful blocks, and they all go together so well!

Materials

Yardage is based on 42"-wide fabric.

1 fat quarter *each* of 18 different floral prints for block centers and pieced center border

1 fat quarter *each* of 18 different coordinating darker prints for baskets and pieced center border

1 fat quarter *each* of 18 different pastel solids or prints for block backgrounds, setting triangles, and inner and outer borders

5¼ yards of fabric for backing

¾ yard total of scraps or printed fabric for binding

71" x 89" piece of batting

Cutting

All measurements include ¼"-wide seam allowances. Please cut all pieces in the order listed.

Inner and Outer Borders

From the pastel solids or prints, cut:

- ❀ 1½"-wide strips to total approximately 270" in length

- ❀ 3"-wide strips to total approximately 300" in length

Blocks

From *each* of the 18 floral prints, cut:

- ❀ 1 square, 8⅜" x 8⅜"; cut each square in half once diagonally to yield 36 half-square triangles (You will use only 18; save the rest for the border or another project.)

From *each* of the 18 coordinating darker prints, cut:

- ❀ 1 square, 8⅜" x 8⅜"; cut each square in half once diagonally to yield 36 half-square triangles. (You will use only 18; save the rest for the border or another project.)

- ❀ 4 squares, 3⅜" x 3⅜"; cut each square in half once diagonally to yield 8 half-square triangles (144 total)

From *each* of the 18 pastel solids or prints, cut:

- ❀ 1 square, 9¾" x 9¾"; cut each square in half once diagonally to yield 36 half-square triangles. (You will use only 24 and have 12 left over.)

- ❀ 1 square, 5⅞" x 5⅞"; cut each square in half once diagonally to yield 36 half-square triangles. (You will use only 18 and have 18 left over.)

- ❀ 2 rectangles, 3" x 8" (36 total)

- ❀ 3 squares, 3⅜" x 3⅜"; cut each square in half once diagonally to yield 108 half-square triangles

- ❀ 1 square, 3" x 3" (18 total)

Pieced Center Border

From the remaining pastel solids or prints, cut:

- ❀ 23 squares, 4¼" x 4¼"; cut each square in half twice diagonally to yield 92 quarter-square triangles

From the remaining floral prints and coordinating darker prints, cut:

- ❀ 11 squares, 7¼" x 7¼"; cut each square in half twice diagonally to yield 44 quarter-square triangles. (You will use only 42 and have 2 left over.)

- ❀ 46 squares, 2⅝" x 2⅝"

Baskets of Flowers *by Terry Martin. Quilted by Barbara Dau. A block exchange*
with my coworkers turned a simple basket block into a quilt with lots of dimension.

Tip When using leftover fabric, make sure to cut along the grain to avoid stretching the edges.

Binding

From the binding fabric, cut:

❀ 2½"-wide strips to total approximately 335" in length

Block Assembly

Since all of the basket blocks are made with different fabrics, the following instructions are for only one block. Create each block from only one floral, one darker print, and one pastel solid or print. Repeat steps 1–5 to make all 18 blocks.

1. Sew the 8⅜" floral triangle to the 8⅜" darker print triangle.

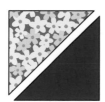

2. Repeat step 1 to pair six 3⅜" darker print triangles with six 3⅜" pastel triangles.

3. Sew three of the half-square-triangle units end to end. Sew the other three half-square-triangle units end to end and sew the 3" pastel square to the end of the unit as shown.

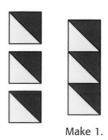

Make 1.

Make 1.

4. Sew the remaining 3⅜" darker print triangles to the ends of the two pastel rectangles.

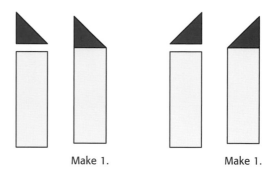

Make 1.   Make 1.

5. Sew together the units from steps 1, 3, and 4, and a 5⅞" pastel half-square triangle to complete a block as shown. Press seam allowances toward the basket fabrics.

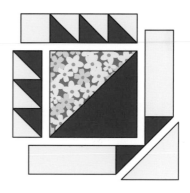

Make 18.

6. Randomly select 20 of the 9¾" pastel half-square triangles and sew them into pairs as shown.

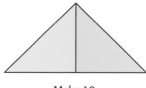

Make 10.

7. Using a design wall or the floor, lay out the blocks in a pleasing arrangement, and then fill in with the setting triangles. Sew the blocks and setting triangles into rows as shown. Sew the rows together.

Border Assembly

1. Sew the 1½"-wide pastel strips together, joining at right angles with a diagonal seam (see page 78). Referring to "Straight-Cut Borders" on page 75, sew the two side borders and then the top and bottom borders to the edges of the quilt top.

2. Sew two 4¼" pastel quarter-square triangles to adjacent sides of a 2⅝" dark square.

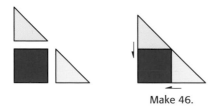

Make 46.

3. Sew the 7¼" floral quarter-square triangles to the units created in step 2 as shown to create the border strips.

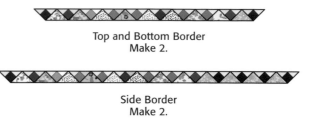

Top and Bottom Border
Make 2.

Side Border
Make 2.

4. Find and mark the center point on each of the border strips and on each edge of the quilt top. From the center point, pin a pieced border strip to the quilt top, working out to the corners and easing along the way. Sew the border strips to each side of the quilt top, stopping ¼" from the corners.

5. Sew the mitered corners by folding the quilt right sides together and aligning the ends of the border strips; stitch from the inside point of the quilt to the outside edge.

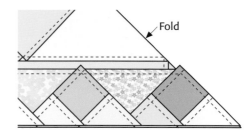

Fold

6. Sew the 3"-wide pastel strips together, joining at right angles with a diagonal seam. Sew the two side borders and then the top and bottom borders to the edges of the quilt top.

Tip Incorporating the scraps from the quilt top into the border is a very cool way to use up the fabrics and give the quilt a bit of a unified look. I also like to piece the binding from the same fabrics to have a scrappy-looking binding if possible!

Finishing

1. Make a quilt sandwich with the quilt top, batting, and backing; for more details on finishing techniques, refer to "Quiltmaking Basics" on page 72. Baste.

2. Quilt as desired. This quilt was quilted by Barbara Dau, a fabulous long-arm machine quilting artist.

She lets the quilt top "talk" to her, and with some input from me, off she goes!

3. Trim the batting and backing even with the edges of the quilt top. Add a hanging sleeve to your quilt if desired.

4. Sew the 2½"-wide binding strips together at right angles with a diagonal seam (see page 78). Sew the binding to the quilt and add a label.

Quilt Plan

Black Beauty

Finished quilt size: 94½" x 94½" ❀ **Finished block sizes:** 4", 12", 24"

*T*his is one of my favorite quilts, and I hope you like it as much as I do. I had a lot of fun "building" this quilt; oddly enough, I started from the outside and worked my way in, knowing that I wanted the center block of this medallion-style quilt to be 24". The challenge I created for myself was that I had to use exclusively black-background floral prints. It was lots of fun auditioning the fabrics so that they would read well against each other.

I consider this a "controlled" scrappy quilt, since it includes 20 different fabrics but each one in a specific area with no repeats. The nature of this quilt lends itself to different cutting and assembly instructions than the other projects in this book. Each set of blocks forming a "round" of the medallion is treated individually regarding fabric quantities, cutting, and assembly. Believe it or not, this quilt is very easy to construct—just work round by round, and as fast as you can say "Black Beauty," you will have a beautiful quilt top! And just to toss in another thought, wouldn't this quilt be great in all white-background floral fabrics?

Tip If you want a more uniform look for the quilt, use the same fabrics in different rounds. To determine how much yardage you will need when repeating a fabric, simply add the required amounts from the different rounds together.

Materials

Yardage is based on 42"-wide fabric. See each of the 8 rounds below for fabric requirements.

Round 1 (24" center block)

½ yard of miniature floral print

¼ yard of large-scale floral print

¼ yard of blue floral print

Scraps or ¼ yard of floral print for center square

Scraps or ¼ yard of pink-green-gold floral print

Scraps or ¼ yard of rose floral print

Round 2 (2" border)

⅜ yard of green leafy floral print

Round 3 (Rail Fence, 4" blocks)

¼ yard *each* of 4 different contrasting floral prints

Round 4 (12" block)

½ yard of floral vine print

½ yard of purple-and-pink floral print

Round 5 (12" block in 2 configurations)

1⅛ yards of small-scale floral print

½ yard of lily floral print

½ yard of pansy floral print

½ yard of miniature-floral print

Round 6 (12" block in 2 configurations)

1⅜ yards of small-scale floral print

⅞ yard of daffodil floral print

¾ yard of dark pink carnation floral print

Round 7 (setting triangles)

1½ yards of mostly black floral print

Round 8 (outer border)

1½ yards of a black-background floral print*

*Or, if you're using a border print, determine the amount needed by measuring through the center of the assembled quilt top from side to side and from top to bottom. (The measurements should be the same since the quilt top is square.) For each side, you'll need 1 of these lengths, plus 2 times the width of the border print, plus ½" for the seam allowances. I usually add about 3" more to be on the safe side.

Black Beauty *by Terry Martin. Quilted by Judy Irish. This striking quilt with all black-background fabrics is fun to make and much easier to stitch up than it looks!*

Additional Fabrics

9 yards of fabric for backing

⅞ yard of fabric for binding

99" x 99" piece of batting (I used black batting)

Cutting and Assembly

I approached the cutting and assembly directions for this project a little differently from the other patterns in the book, grouping the directions together by rounds. Because I created the quilt in rounds, it was important for me to audition fabrics from one completed round to the next. This way I avoided making mistakes in fabric selection, since fabrics often look good as a group but when you put them side by side, they don't always work out. Instead of cutting everything up front, I found it helpful to create round one, the center block, and then audition the border fabric next to it. Then I auditioned round two fabrics against round three fabrics, and so on. This way I was able to create the secondary designs with greater success. Take it one round at a time and watch your quilt grow!

Note that you'll assemble blocks for rounds four through six and then set them aside until round seven, when you'll join them to the pieces from rounds one through three to make the quilt top. The border is added in round eight.

Round 1 (24" center block)

From the pink-green-gold floral print, cut:

❀ 4 squares, 3⅞" x 3⅞"; cut each square in half once diagonally to yield 8 half-square triangles

From the blue floral print, cut:

❀ 1 square, 7¼" x 7¼"; cut the square in half twice diagonally to yield 4 quarter-square triangles

❀ 4 squares, 3½" x 3½"

From the floral print for center, cut:

❀ 1 square, 6½" x 6½" (I fussy cut this bouquet of flowers.)

From the miniature-floral print, cut:

❀ 16 squares, 3⅞" x 3⅞"; cut each square in half once diagonally to yield 32 half-square triangles

❀ 8 squares, 3½" x 3½"

From the rose floral print, cut:

❀ 8 squares, 3⅞" x 3⅞"; cut each square in half once diagonally to yield 16 half-square triangles

From the large-scale floral print, cut:

❀ 4 squares, 6⅞" x 6⅞"; cut each square in half once diagonally to yield 8 half-square triangles

1. Sew a pink-green-gold floral triangle to the two short sides of each blue floral triangle.

Make 4.

2. Sew two of the units from step 1 to opposite sides of the 6½" center square.

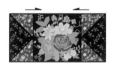

3. Sew the blue floral squares to each end of the remaining units created in step 1.

4. Sew the units from step 3 to the remaining sides of the block center.

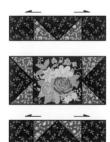 

Make 1.

5. Sew a miniature-floral triangle to each of the rose floral triangles.

Make 16.

6. Pair eight of the half-square-triangle units from step 5 with the 3½" miniature-floral squares and then join the resulting units as shown.

Make 4.

7. Sew the remaining miniature-floral triangles to two adjacent sides of each remaining half-square-triangle unit.

Make 8.

8. Sew the large-scale floral triangles to the units created in step 7 and then sew these units together into pairs as shown.

 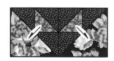

Make 4.

9. Sew two of the units created in step 8 to opposite sides of the block center.

10. Sew the units created in step 6 to each end of the remaining units from step 8.

Make 2.

11. Sew these units to opposite sides of the block center.

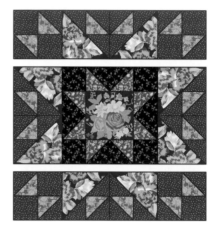

Round 2 (2" border)

From the green leafy floral print, cut:

❀ 2 strips, 2½" x 24½"

❀ 2 strips, 2½" x 28½"

Sew the two shorter strips to opposite sides of the center square. Sew the two longer strips to the remaining sides of the center square.

Round 3 (Rail Fence, 4" block)

From *each* of the 4 different floral prints, cut:

❀ 4 strips, 1½" x 42"

1. Sew together four strips, one of each print, in whatever order you prefer. Repeat to make four strip sets.

2. Crosscut the strip sets into 32 segments, 4½" wide.

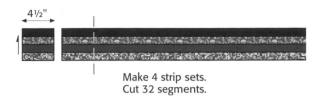

Make 4 strip sets.
Cut 32 segments.

3. Make two Rail Fence strips by sewing seven of the segments together as shown. Make two more Rail Fence strips by sewing nine of the segments together as shown.

Make 2.

Make 2.

4. Sew the shorter strips to opposite sides of the quilt center, taking care to orient the strips as shown. Sew the longer strips to the two remaining sides, orienting the strips as shown.

Round 4 (12" block)

From the floral vine print, cut:

❀ 8 squares, 3½" x 3½"
❀ 16 rectangles, 3½" x 6½"

From the purple-and-pink floral print, cut:

❀ 24 squares, 3½" x 3½"

1. Sew two squares from each print together to make four-patch units.

2. Sew a vine print rectangle to the top and bottom of each four-patch unit.

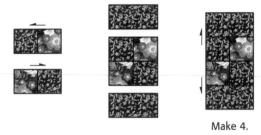

Make 4.

3. Sew the remaining purple-and-pink floral squares to each end of the remaining vine print rectangles. Sew these units to the sides of each block center. Set these blocks aside.

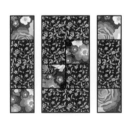 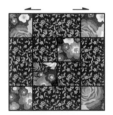

Make 4.

Round 5 (12" block in 2 configurations)

From the small-scale floral print, cut:

❀ 7 strips, 2" x 42"
❀ 6 strips, 3½" x 42"; crosscut into 64 squares, 3½" x 3½"

From the miniature-floral print, cut:

❀ 7 strips, 2" x 42"

From the lily floral print, cut:

❧ 8 squares, 6½" x 6½"

From the pansy floral print, cut:

❧ 8 squares, 6½" x 6½"

1. Sew each 2" x 42" small-scale floral strip to a 2" x 42" miniature-floral strip to make seven strip sets. Crosscut the strip sets into 128 segments, 2" wide.

Make 7 strip sets.
Cut 128 segments.

2. Sew the segments from step 1 together in pairs to make 64 four-patch units.

3. Sew a 3½" small-scale floral square to one side of each four-patch unit.

Make 64.

4. Sew the units from step 3 into pairs as shown.

Make 32.

5. Sew 16 of the units from step 4 together in groups of four to create the corner blocks.

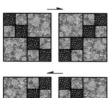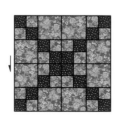

Make 4.

6. Sew the 6½" squares of pansy print to one side of eight of the remaining blocks from step 4. Sew the 6½" squares of pansy print to one side of the remaining eight squares. Sew the resulting units together in pairs as shown to make eight blocks. Set these blocks aside.

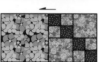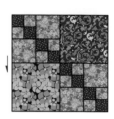

Make 8.

Round 6 (12" block in 2 configurations)

From the dark pink carnation floral print, cut:

❧ 4 strips, 2½" x 42"

❧ 2 strips, 4½" x 42"

From the daffodil floral print, cut:

❧ 2 strips, 4½" x 42"

❧ 6 strips, 2½" x 42"

From the small-scale floral print, cut:

❧ 8 strips, 2½" x 42"; crosscut into 32 rectangles, 2½" x 8½"

❧ 2 strips, 10½" x 42"

1. Sew a 2½"-wide strip of the carnation floral to opposite long sides of both 4½"-wide daffodil floral strips to make two strip sets. Crosscut these strip sets into 16 segments, 4½" wide.

Make 2 strip sets.
Cut 16 segments.

2. Sew a 2½"-wide strip of the daffodil floral to opposite long sides of both 4½"-wide carnation floral strips to make two strip sets. Crosscut these strip sets into 32 segments, 2½" wide.

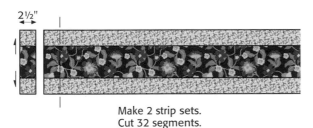

Make 2 strip sets.
Cut 32 segments.

3. Sew the segments from step 2 to opposite sides of the segments from step 1.

Make 16.

4. Sew the 2½" x 8½" small-scale floral rectangles to opposite sides of each unit created in step 3.

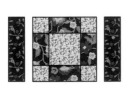 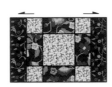

5. Sew a 2½"-wide strip of the daffodil floral to one long side of both 10½"-wide small-scale floral strips. Crosscut into 32 segments, 2½" wide.

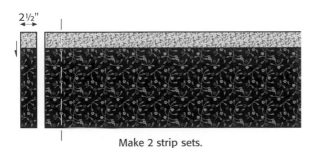

Make 2 strip sets.
Cut 32 segments.

6. Sew the segments from step 5 to the units from step 4 as shown to make two different block configurations. Set the blocks aside.

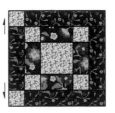 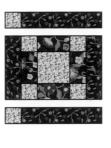

Make 4.

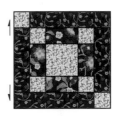 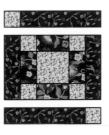

Make 12.

Round 7 (setting triangles)

From the mostly black floral print, cut:

❀ 2 strips, 18¼" x 42"; crosscut into 4 squares, 18¼" x 18¼". Cut each square in half twice diagonally to yield 16 quarter-square triangles.

❀ 1 strip, 9⅜" x 42"; crosscut into 2 squares, 9⅜" x 9⅜". Cut each square in half once diagonally to yield 4 half-square triangles.

1. Using all of the blocks from rounds 4–6 and the setting triangles that you have already cut for round 7, lay out the rows in units A and B as shown on page 62. Sew the blocks and setting triangles in each of the rows together.

2. Sew the rows together to create two each of units A and B as shown.

3. Sew the unit A pieces to opposite sides of the quilt center. Sew the unit B pieces to opposite sides of the resulting unit.

Round 8 (outer border)

From the black-background floral print, cut:

❀ 9 strips, 5" x 42"*

Or, if you are using a border print, measure through the center of the quilt both ways. (The measurements should be the same since the quilt top is square.) You will need one of these lengths, plus two times the width of the border print, plus ½" for the seam allowances for each of the four sides. I usually add 3" more to be on the safe side. The width of the outside border on the quilt shown was dictated only by the print on the fabric, so if you find a border print of a different width that you like, go ahead and use it.

Referring to "Borders" on pages 75–76, add the outer border to the quilt top. If you are using a border print, follow the directions for "Borders with Mitered Corners." If you have chosen a nonborder print for the outer border, you do not have to make mitered corners; follow the instructions for "Straight-Cut Borders."

Quilt Assembly Diagram

Finishing

1. Make a quilt sandwich with the quilt top, batting, and backing; for more details on finishing techniques, refer to "Quiltmaking Basics" on page 72. Baste.

2. Quilt as desired. Judy Irish is a professional machine quilter and a member of my quilt guild. When I saw her trunk show at one of our meetings, I asked if she would be interested in working on one of my quilts for this book. Her work was great, but even more appealing was her sense of humor. When she took a look at my quilt top I could see her creative juices bubbling! I have to admit I am a little jealous. Even though people "ooh" and "aah" when they first see my quilt, they become truly stunned when they examine the beautiful quilting Judy added.

3. Trim the batting and backing even with the edges of the quilt top. Add a hanging sleeve to your quilt if desired.

4. From the binding fabric, cut 10 strips, 2½" x 42".

5. Sew the 2½" x 42" binding strips together at right angles with a diagonal seam (see page 78). Sew the binding to the quilt and add a label.

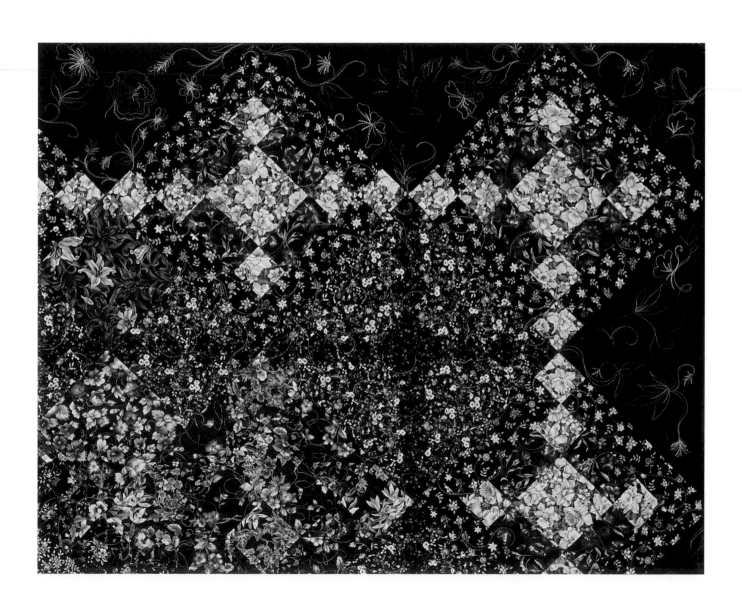

Retro Rhapsody

Finished quilt size: 84¾" x 94¼" ❁ **Finished block size:** 9½"

*T*he feature fabric in this quilt reminds me of my grandmother's curtains from the 1950s. She was quite a quilter in her own right, although she never followed any of the quilting rules. Grandma Maxwell was a utilitarian quilter: she only quilted during the winter months when she couldn't be out in her enormous garden, and she made do with what she had. Her crazy quilts were stitched together from leftover garment fabric, my grandpa's work clothes and nightshirts, and whatever else she could get a hold of, including double-knit polyester!

She'd piece these random fabrics together, tie the layers, then simply fold in the edges and sew a running stitch along the outside. (Why bother with a binding? These were working quilts made to be used, and used up.) The first time they went through the wash the batting would pile up in several large lumps, but we loved getting them for presents.

I have several of these quilts that have lasted through years of being hauled to picnics and the beach. One adorned the end of my bed at college, and my 17-year-old daughter now has the same quilt folded up at the end of her bed.

Materials

Yardage is based on 42"-wide fabric.

3½ yards of teal floral print for blocks, borders, and binding

⅞ yard *each* of 9 assorted fabrics for blocks and borders, in light to dark values that coordinate with the teal floral

⅜ yard of purple fabric for cornerstones

7¾ yards of fabric for backing

89" x 98" piece of batting

Cutting

All measurements include ¼"-wide seam allowances.

From the teal floral print and each of the 9 coordinating fabrics, cut:

❀ 3 strips, 5½" x 42"; crosscut into:
6 squares, 5½" x 5½" (60 total)
12 rectangles, 2¾" x 5½" (120 total)
18 rectangles, 1½" x 5½" (180 total)

❀ 1 strip, 10" x 42"; crosscut into 12 rectangles, 2¾" x 10" (120 total)

From the teal floral print, make these additional cuts:

❀ 8 strips, 2" x 42"

❀ 10 binding strips, 2½" x 42"

❀ 4 strips, 9⅜" x 42"

❀ 4 squares, 5" x 5"; cut each square in half once diagonally to make 8 half-square triangles

❀ 1 square, 8" x 8"; cut the square in half twice diagonally to make 4 quarter-square triangles

From the purple fabric, cut:

❀ 1 strip, 9⅜" x 42"; crosscut into 4 squares, 9⅜" x 9⅜"

Assembly

1. Randomly pair up the 5½" center squares with 2¾" x 5½" and 2¾" x 10" rectangles of a coordinating fabric.

2. Sew the small rectangles to the top and bottom of the center squares.

3. Sew the large rectangles to the remaining sides of the units from step 2.

Make 60.

Retro Rhapsody *by Terry Martin. Quilted by Sue Lohse. This is another "blast from the past" quilt for me, featuring a floral print that is reminiscent of vintage curtains in my childhood home.*

4. On your design wall (the living room floor also works great!), arrange the blocks in eight rows of seven blocks each. (You will have four extra blocks, allowing you a bit of freedom when searching for that perfect arrangement. You may wish to trim these leftovers down and use them in the corners of the quilt, or use one for the label on the back, or use them to make matching pillows.) Sew the blocks into rows, pressing seam allowances in opposite directions from row to row. Then sew the rows together to complete the center of the quilt.

5. Sew the 1½" x 5½" rectangles of coordinating fabric in a random order to the short sides of each of the teal floral quarter-square triangles as shown. Add a total of 45 strips to each triangle to create a chevron pattern. Press the seam allowances toward the strips.

Add 45 strips.
Make 4.

Tip Alternate between finger-pressing and pressing with an iron. You can get away with pressing about four or five strip seams with your fingers before you need to press with an iron.

6. Sew the teal floral half-square triangles to each side of the pointed end of the chevron units you created in step 5. Press the seam allowances toward the triangles.

7. Center each chevron unit under a clear grid ruler and trim the sides so the unit measures 6⅜" wide.

8. Measure the length of the chevron units and trim the 2"-wide strips of teal floral to this measured length. Sew the strips to each side of the chevron units.

6⅜"

9. Measure the quilt top through the center in both directions. Subtract the length of the chevrons from the quilt top measurements and add ½" for seam allowances. Trim two 9⅜" x 42" strips to each of the determined measurements. Sew the strips to the ends of the corresponding chevron units.

10. Sew the two side border units to the quilt top. Press the seams toward the borders.

11. Sew the 9⅜" purple squares to each end of the top and bottom border units.

12. Sew the top and bottom borders to the quilt top. Press the seams toward the border.

Quilt Plan

Finishing

1. Make a quilt sandwich with the quilt top, batting, and backing; for more details on finishing techniques, refer to "Quiltmaking Basics" on page 72. Baste.

2. Quilt as desired. Whew!—This quilt has a lot of squares. I asked my machine-quilting friend Sue Lohse to give it some curves, so she gently meandered across the face of the quilt and used a neutral thread color. The effect gives extra softness to the quilt's many angles.

3. Trim the batting and backing even with the edges of the quilt top. Add a hanging sleeve to your quilt if desired.

4. Sew the 2½" x 42" teal floral strips together at right angles with a diagonal seam (see page 78) for the binding. Sew the binding to the quilt and add a label.

Passion Flower

Finished quilt size: 93" x 107" ✿ **Finished block size:** 10"

*C*heck out the scale of the print in this feature fabric. Is it wild or what! I know I have said it before, but I am constantly amazed at what the fabric makers come up with on a regular basis. This is a Woodrow Studio fabric; that company produced a number of huge floral prints as a collection and I love them. The pansies in this print are as big as a dinner plate. You can probably guess why I chose a 4" sashing and a large plain border—the fabric speaks (or perhaps shouts) for itself. Have fun with outrageously large-scale prints!

Materials

Yardage is based on 42"-wide fabric.

6½ yards of purple pansy print for sashing, outer border, and binding

15 coordinating fat quarters for blocks

½ yard of green print for inner border

8½ yards of fabric for backing

97" x 111" piece of batting

Cutting

All measurements include ¼"-wide seam allowances.

From *each* coordinating fat quarter, cut:

- ❁ 4 squares, 5⅞" x 5⅞"; cut each square in half once diagonally to yield 8 half-square triangles (120 total)

- ❁ 3 strips, 2¼" x 18"; crosscut into 24 squares, 2¼" x 2¼" (360 total)*

- ❁ 8 additional squares, 2¼" x 2¼" (120 total)*

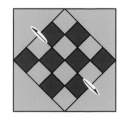

* You may want to consider keeping the 2¼" strips intact, and instead use strip piecing to create the center of the blocks.

From the purple pansy print, cut:

- ❁ 3 strips, 10½" x 42"; crosscut the strips into 24 rectangles, 4½" x 10½"

- ❁ 9 strips, 4½" x 42"

- ❁ 9 strips, 12½" x 42"

- ❁ 11 strips, 2½" x 42"

From the green print, cut:

- ❁ 8 strips, 1¾" x 42"

Assembly

1. Select eight 2¼" squares from each of two coordinating fabrics for the checkerboard center of the block. Make a total of 30 block centers.

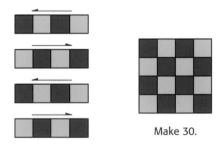

Make 30.

2. Select four half-square triangles that match one of the coordinating fabrics from the block center and sew the triangles to the sides of the block center.

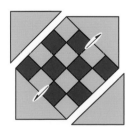

Make 30.

Passion Flower by Terry Martin. Quilted by Kathryn Milburn.
I know the pansy is not a real passion flower, but I named this quilt for my
dad. He always called my mother Passion Flower and he loved brilliant colors.

3. Sew a 4½" x 10½" pansy print rectangle to the right side of 24 blocks.

 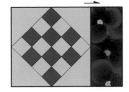

Make 24.

4. Select six units from step 3 and sew one of the remaining six blocks to the sashing side of the units.

Make 6.

5. Sew three of the units from step 3 and one of the units from step 4 together to make six rows of five blocks each.

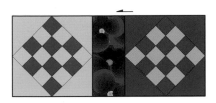

Make 6.

6. Sew the 4½"-wide pansy print strips end to end and crosscut into five sashing strips, each 4½" x 66½".

7. Sew a sashing strip to the bottom of five of the rows of blocks.

8. Sew the block-and-sashing rows together and add the remaining block row to the bottom of the quilt center.

9. Referring to "Straight-Cut Borders" on page 75, measure, trim, and sew the green print strips for the side inner borders to the quilt top first and then repeat for the top and bottom inner borders.

Repeat for the 12½"-wide pansy print outer-border strips.

Quilt Plan

Finishing

1. Make a quilt sandwich with the quilt top, batting, and backing; for more details on finishing techniques, refer to "Quiltmaking Basics" on page 72. Baste.

2. Quilt as desired. Kathryn Milburn quilted this quilt and she had a lot of fun with the large print. I asked her to use a lightweight batting because I plan to use it as a summer quilt. The extra loft of the polyester batting gave the flowers more dimension when Kathy outline stitched them in the border.

3. Trim the batting and backing even with the edges of the quilt top. Add a hanging sleeve to your quilt if desired.

4. Sew the 2½" x 42" pansy print strips together at right angles with a diagonal seam (see page 78) for the binding. Sew the binding to the quilt and add a label.

Quiltmaking Basics

This section provides you with all the necessary elements for successfully completing your project, from choosing fabric and assembling essential tools for quiltmaking, to chain piecing, pressing, adding borders, making a quilt sandwich, quilting, binding, and finally, adding a hanging sleeve and label.

Fabrics

My grandmother called fabric "material," and so did I until the eighties. (I think I just dated myself!) I would watch her finger the cloth for smoothness and drape and then pass her entire hand over the surface as if communicating with it. Watching her make clothes for our large family gave me a real sense of pride. Who needed store-bought clothes when I had a one-of-a-kind dress to wear on my first day of school? Later I found out that I was wearing haute couture before I knew how fashionable it was! For me, fabric is the stuff of life and has been for as long as I can remember. Buy fabric, make things, and enjoy your accomplishments.

For quilting I use 100%-cotton fabric. I try to buy the best quality cotton my budget can afford, but that doesn't mean I don't look through the bargain bins. Some of my favorite fabrics are the inexpensive finds. Many people think that the cheaper fabrics won't last as long, and I can't tell you whether that is true or not. It is my philosophy that it's OK if my quilts don't last for generations. I want my quilts loved, used, and used up. I have the privilege of being able to make many, many quilts; some will survive and some won't. This thinking is very freeing for me, giving me the opportunity to use what I want, even when it came from the bargain bin.

Yardage requirements are provided for all projects in this book and are based on 40" of usable fabric.

To prewash or not to prewash, that is the question, and it's one that sparks constant debate among quilters. I don't prewash my fabric unless I am using muslin or flannel. Instead of going into the reasons why I don't prewash, I would like to leave it up to the individual. Whatever you are comfortable doing, do it!

Tip

I am always amazed when I show my quilts and the audience wants to see the back of the quilt. They usually want to see how the machine quilting looks, but they always comment on the fabric. How could I use such beautiful fabric for the back of a quilt! I try to match the back of the quilt to the theme or color of the front, but it doesn't always happen. I have the luxury of using great fabric on the back of the quilt because I am diligent about shopping the fabric sale rack. These are usually nice-quality cotton goods that just didn't sell. I buy 5 to 10 yards off a bolt just to be used for backings. This way I always have it on hand and it usually cost me a fraction of the original price.

Supplies

- **Sewing machine:** You will need a sewing machine that has a good straight stitch. You'll also need a walking foot or darning foot if you are going to machine quilt. Take a moment to clean and oil your machine, and try to get into the practice of cleaning your machine before every project. Cotton is a great fiber but it does create lint under the feed dogs, which can interfere with the smooth running of your sewing machine.

- **Rotary-cutting tools:** You will need a rotary cutter, cutting mat, and clear acrylic ruler. The 6" x 24" size works well for cutting long strips and squares. You should also have a large square ruler for squaring up quilt blocks.

- **Thread:** Use a good-quality, all-purpose cotton or cotton-covered polyester thread. Choose a neutral color such as gray, because it won't show through when you are piecing light and dark fabrics together.

❖ **Basic sewing tools:** You will need needles for both hand and machine sewing, pins, and fabric scissors for cutting threads. Don't forget the seam ripper, the smaller the better so the point can slide through the stitches easily. You will need an iron and ironing board for pressing seams, and tracing tools such as pencil and paper for the appliqué projects.

❖ **Double-backed fusible webbing:** I use Steam-A-Seam 2 by the Warm Company. It holds very well and adds just enough body to the fabric, without stiffness, that I generally don't have to use a stabilizer when I machine blanket stitch around the edges of fused designs.

Rotary Cutting

All of the projects are designed for quick-and-easy rotary cutting except those involving fusible appliqué. All measurements except the templates include standard ¼"-wide seam allowances. Here is a quick lesson on rotary cutting.

1. Fold the fabric and match the selvages, aligning the crosswise and lengthwise grains as much as possible. Place the folded edge closest to you on the cutting mat. Align a square ruler along the folded edge of the fabric. Then place a long, straight ruler to the left of the square ruler, just covering the uneven raw edges of the left side of the fabric.

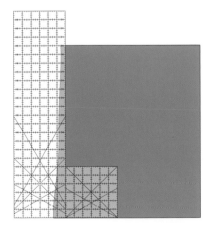

Remove the square ruler and cut along the right edge of the long ruler, rolling the rotary cutter away from you. Discard this strip. (Reverse this procedure if you are left-handed.)

2. To cut strips, align the required measurement on the ruler with the newly cut edge of the fabric. For example, to cut a 3"-wide strip, place the 3" ruler mark on the edge of the fabric.

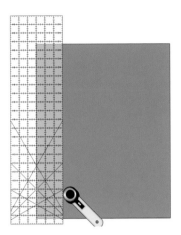

3. To cut squares, cut strips in the required widths. Trim away the selvage ends of the strip. Align the required measurement on the ruler with the left edge of the strip and cut a square. Continue cutting squares until you have the number you need.

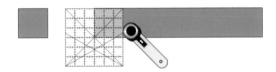

Machine Piecing

The most important thing to remember about machine piecing is to maintain a consistent scant ¼"-wide seam allowance. Some sewing machines have a special ¼" foot that measures exactly ¼" from the center needle position to the edge of the foot. This feature allows you to use the edge of the presser foot to guide the fabric for a perfect ¼"-wide seam allowance.

If your machine doesn't have such a foot, create a seam guide by placing the edge of a piece of tape ¼" from the needle.

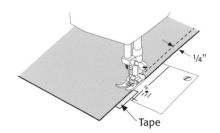

Chain Piecing

Chain piecing is an efficient, timesaving system.

1. Sew the first pair of pieces from cut edge to cut edge, using about 12 stitches per inch. At the end of the seam, stop sewing, but do not cut the thread.

2. Feed the next pair of pieces under the presser foot, as close as possible to the first pair. Continue feeding pieces through the machine without cutting the thread in between. There is no need to backstitch, since each seam will be crossed and held by another seam.

3. When all pieces have been sewn, remove the chain from the machine and clip the threads between pieces.

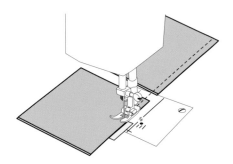

Easing

If two pieces that will be sewn together differ slightly in size (by less than ⅛"), pin the places where the two pieces should match. Next pin the middle, if necessary, to distribute the excess fabric evenly. Sew the seam with the longer piece on the bottom, next to the feed dogs. The feed dogs will help ease the two pieces together.

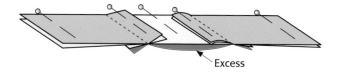

Excess

Pressing

Pressing is very important for many reasons. It helps sink the thread into the fabric, it sets the seam, and it helps you see if the pieces are stitched accurately. Remember that pressing and ironing are two different things. While pressing, use an up-and-down motion and avoid sliding the iron back and forth over a block. This will help prevent distortion. I use both a dry iron and steam, depending on how the fabric reacts to the different types of heat. Make sure the iron face is clean.

The traditional rule in quiltmaking is to press seams to one side, toward the darker color wherever possible. Press the seam flat from the wrong side first, and then press the seam in the desired direction from the right side. Be particularly careful when pressing bias seams or edges.

When joining two seamed units, plan ahead and press the seam allowances in opposite directions as shown. This reduces bulk and makes it easier to match seam lines. Where two seams meet, the seam allowances will butt against each other, making it easier to join units with perfectly matched seam intersections.

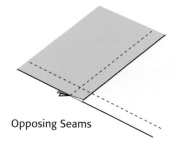

Opposing Seams

Appliqué

I want my projects to be quick and easy, so I use double-backed fusible webbing for the appliqué projects in this book. Please use your favorite appliqué method. The templates that are provided for each of the projects do not have seam allowances.

If you do use double-backed fusible webbing, follow the directions on the package. For any project that will be handled a lot, you will need to anchor the edges of the appliqué so they won't lift up with repeated washing. I use my sewing machine's preprogrammed blanket stitch to secure the appliqué to the background fabric. You can also use a blind hem stitch or satin stitch by machine.

Blanket Stitch

Blind Hem Stitch

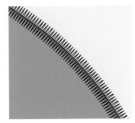
Satin Stitch

Borders

For best results, do not cut border strips and sew them directly to the quilt sides without measuring first, unless the quilt is small like a wall hanging. The edges of a quilt often measure slightly longer than the distance through the quilt center, due to stretching during construction. Instead, measure the quilt top through the center in both directions to determine how long to cut the border strips. Then sew the strips to the edges of the quilt, easing to fit. This step ensures that the finished quilt will be as straight and as "square" as possible, without wavy edges.

Plain border strips are cut along the crosswise grain and seamed where extra length is needed.

Straight-Cut Borders

All of the borders in this book are either straight-cut borders or have details of one kind or another. For the detailed borders please follow the directions given with the individual project. For straight-cut borders:

1. Measure the length of the quilt top through the center. Cut border strips to that measurement, piecing as necessary; mark the center of the quilt edges and the border strips. Pin the borders to the sides of the quilt top, matching the center marks

and ends and easing as necessary. Sew the border strips in place. Press seams toward the border.

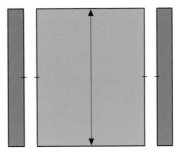
Measure center of quilt,
top to bottom.
Mark centers.

2. Measure the width of the quilt top through the center, including the side borders just added. Cut border strips to that measurement, piecing as necessary; mark the center of the quilt edges and the border strips. Pin the borders to the top and bottom edges of the quilt top, matching the center marks and ends and easing as necessary; stitch. Press seams toward the border.

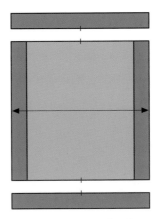
Measure center of quilt,
side to side, including borders.
Mark centers.

Borders with Mitered Corners

1. Cut the border strips as indicated in the project directions and mark the centers with a pin. Mark the center of the quilt edges with pins.

2. Measure the length and width of the quilt top through the center in both directions and record the measurements. Place a pin at each end of the side border strips to indicate the length of the quilt top. Repeat with the top and bottom border strips.

3. Pin the side borders to the quilt top, matching the pin marks at the centers and matching the pins at the ends of the border strip with the edges of the quilt top. Stitch, beginning and ending stitching ¼" from the raw edges of the quilt top. Repeat with the top and bottom border strips.

4. Lay one corner of the quilt top on the ironing board. Fold under one border strip at a 45° angle to the other strip. Press and pin.

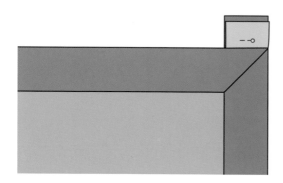

5. Fold the quilt, right sides together, and line up the edges of the border strips. Stitch along the pressed crease, sewing from the inner corner to the outer edge. Trim the seam allowance to ¼" and press the seam open. Miter the remaining corners in the same manner.

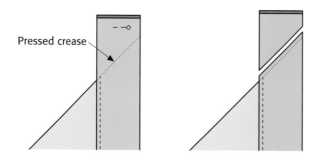

Pressed crease

Marking the Quilting Lines

Whether or not to mark the quilting designs depends upon the type of quilting you will be doing. Marking is not necessary if you plan to quilt in the ditch or outline quilt a uniform distance from seam lines. For more complex quilting designs, mark the quilt top before the quilt is layered with batting and backing.

Choose a marking tool that will be visible on your fabric and test it on fabric scraps to be sure the marks can be removed easily.

I use blue painter's tape for straight-line quilting. This tape is designed not to leave a sticky residue on your walls—or on your quilt! You can find painter's tape at your local hardware store, and it comes in a variety of widths. By using both edges of the tape you can achieve both better speed and a great appearance in your quilting.

Layering the Quilt

The quilt "sandwich" consists of backing, batting, and the quilt top. Cut the quilt backing at least 4" larger in both length and width than the quilt top. For large quilts, it is usually necessary to sew two or three lengths of fabric together to make a backing of the required size. Trim away the selvages before piecing the lengths together. Press seams open to make quilting easier.

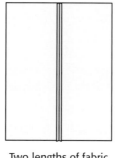

Two lengths of fabric seamed in the center

1 fabric width

Partial fabric width

Batting comes packaged in standard bed sizes, or it can be purchased by the yard. Several weights or thicknesses are available. Thick battings are fine for tied quilts and comforters; a thinner batting is better, however, if you intend to quilt by hand or machine.

To put it all together:

1. Spread the backing, wrong side up, on a flat, clean surface. Anchor it with pins or masking tape. Be careful not to stretch the backing out of shape.

2. Spread the batting over the backing, smoothing out any wrinkles.

3. Place the pressed quilt top on top of the batting. Smooth out any wrinkles and make sure the quilt-top edges are parallel to the edges of the backing.

4. Starting in the center, baste with needle and thread and work diagonally to each corner. Continue

basting in a grid of horizontal and vertical lines 6" to 8" apart. Finish by basting around the edges.

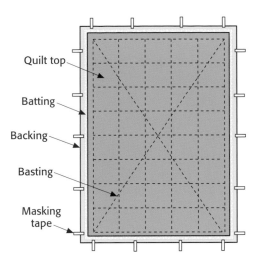

Quilt top

Batting

Backing

Basting

Masking tape

Note: For machine quilting, you may baste the layers with rustproof safety pins. Place pins about 6" to 8" apart, away from the area you intend to quilt.

For small projects that I plan to machine quilt I also use a spray adhesive to anchor the layers together with a lot of success! There are several brands available on the market but my favorite is 505 Spray, which doesn't have toxic fumes and works very well.

Machine Quilting

Machine quilting is suitable for all types of quilts, from crib to full-size bed quilts. With machine quilting, you can quickly complete quilts and start that next project that is calling out to you.

Marking is only necessary if you need to follow a grid or a complex pattern. It is not necessary if you plan to quilt in the ditch, outline quilt a uniform distance from seam lines, or free-motion quilt in a random pattern over the quilt surface or in selected areas.

1. For straight-line quilting, it is extremely helpful to have a walking foot to help feed the quilt layers through the machine without shifting or pucker-

ing. Some machines have a built-in walking foot; other machines require a separate attachment.

Walking Foot

Quilting in the Ditch

Outline Quilting

2. For free-motion quilting, you need a darning foot and the ability to drop the feed dogs on your machine. With free-motion quilting, you do not turn the fabric under the needle but instead guide the fabric in the direction of the design. Use free-motion quilting to outline quilt a fabric motif or to create stippling or other curved designs.

Darning Foot

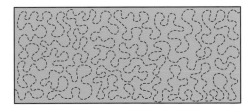

Free-Motion Quilting

Binding

Bindings can be made from straight-grain or bias strips of fabric. All of the quilts in this book call for a French double-fold binding.

To cut straight-grain binding strips, cut 2½"-wide strips across the width of the fabric. You will need enough strips to go around the perimeter of the quilt plus 10" for seams and the corners in a mitered fold.

1. Sew strips, right sides together, to make one long piece of binding. Join strips at right angles and stitch across the corner as shown. Trim excess fabric and press the seams open.

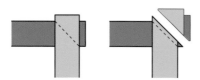

Joining Straight-Cut Strips

2. Fold the strip in half lengthwise, wrong sides together, and press. Unfold one end and trim at a 45° angle; turn under ¼" and press. Turning the end under at an angle distributes the bulk so you won't have a lump where the two ends of the binding meet.

Fold line

3. Trim the batting and backing even with the quilt top. If you plan to add a hanging sleeve, do so now before attaching the binding (see page 79).

4. Starting on one side of the quilt and using a ¼"-wide seam allowance, stitch the binding to the quilt, keeping the raw edges even with the quilt-top edge. End the stitching ¼" from the corner of the quilt and backstitch. Clip the thread.

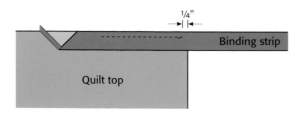

¼"

Binding strip

Quilt top

5. Turn the quilt so that you'll be stitching down the next side. Fold the binding up, away from the quilt, and then back down onto itself, parallel with the edge of the quilt top. Begin stitching at the edge, backstitching to secure. Repeat on the remaining edges and corners of the quilt.

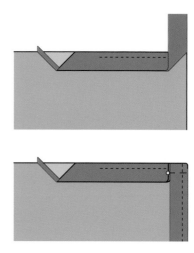

6. When you reach the beginning of the binding, overlap the beginning stitches by 1" and cut away any excess binding, trimming the end at a 45° angle. Tuck the end of the binding into the fold and finish the seam.

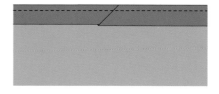

7. Fold the binding over the raw edges of the quilt to the back, with the folded edge covering the row of machine stitching, and blindstitch in place. A miter will form at each corner. Blindstitch the mitered corners.

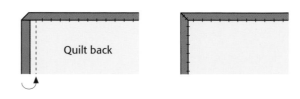

Quilt back

Adding a Sleeve

If you plan to display your finished quilt on the wall, be sure to add a hanging sleeve to hold the rod.

1. Using leftover fabric from the quilt front or a piece of muslin, cut a strip 6" to 8" wide and 1" shorter than the width of the quilt at the top edge. Fold the ends under ½", and then ½" again; stitch.

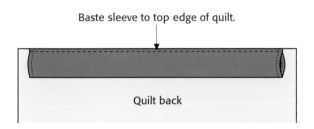

2. Fold the fabric in half lengthwise, wrong sides together, and baste the raw edges to the top edge of the quilt back. The top edge of the sleeve will be secured when the binding is sewn on the quilt.

Baste sleeve to top edge of quilt.

Quilt back

3. Finish the sleeve after the binding has been attached by blindstitching the bottom of the sleeve in place. Push the bottom edge of the sleeve up just a bit to provide a little give so the hanging rod does not put strain on the quilt itself.

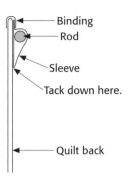

Binding
Rod
Sleeve
Tack down here.

Quilt back

Signing Your Quilt

Be sure to sign and date your quilt. Future generations will be interested to know more than just who made it and when. Labels can be as elaborate or as simple as you desire. The information can be handwritten, typed, or embroidered. Be sure to include the name of the quilt, your name, your city and state, the date, the name of the recipient if it is a gift, and any other interesting or important information about the quilt.

About the Author

Terry Martin was born and raised in the Pacific Northwest and couldn't imagine living anywhere else. She has been seriously quilting for about eight years, and before that she was an avid cross-stitcher, a dabbler in crewel and embroidery work, and the maker of most of her own clothes.

Terry's family is her pride and joy, and she relishes the fact that her grandmother played a large role in her love of fabric and textile art. One of her sisters, Glenda, has been bitten by the quilting bug, and although the other members of the family—including siblings, nieces, nephews, daughter McKenzie, and husband Ed—do not sew, they truly know what goes into a quilt, and they cherish what is made for them. Actually, her husband claims he is going to take a sewing class and learn to make quilts (he already has his own fabric stash).

This is Terry's fourth quilting book, and she has many more ideas than time. She loves to lecture and teach classes, and she hopes to eventually translate more of her quilting ideas into books.